A Southern Sampler

Art • Poetry • Stories • Recipes

COMPILED BY

Southern Sampler Artists Colony

ILLUSTRATIONS BY Tim Mitoma

Southern Sampler Artists Colony Press
San Rafael • California

For permission to print essays, poems, art or recipes in this volume, acknowledgement is made to the holders of copyright named on pages 188-199.

Grateful acknowledgement is made to the following for permission to reprint from previously published material:
Linda Watanabe McFerrin, *Southern Exposure: On the Palmetto Trail*, first published in *San Francisco Chronicle Magazine*, San Francisco, California; Linda Watanabe McFerrin, *A Low Country B'al*, first published in *Rocky Mountain News*, Denver, Colorado; Charlotte Jenkins, *Country Ham and Gravy* from *Gullah Cuisine: By Land and By Sea*, reprinted by permission, *Evening Post Books*, Charleston, South Carolina; Joanna Crowell, poems: *Landing, How Will She Know, Johns Island SC, Blurred Borders, My Love Is*, from *I Ate a Rainbow for Breakfast* reprinted by permission, *WordofMouth Books*, Charleston, South Carolina; Jack McCray, *The Golden Age of Jazz in Charleston*, reprinted by permission, *JAZZ! Art Quilts in Performance*, Charleston Jazz Initiative, College of Charleston, Charleston, South Carolina; Marlene O'Bryant Seabrook, *Dizzy* reprinted by permission, *JAZZ! Art Quilts in Performance*, Charleston Jazz Initiative, College of Charleston, Charleston, South Carolina; Alphonso Brown, *93 Anson Street*, from *A Gullah Guide to Charleston—Walking Through Black History*, reprinted by permission, *The History Press*, Charleston, South Carolina; *Jenkins Orphanage photograph* reprinted by permission, *Charleston Jazz*, Jack McCray, Charleston Jazz Initiative, Charleston, South Carolina; Linda Ferguson, poems: *Art Therapy, Low Tide, The Question*, reprinted by permission, *Word Tech Editions*, Charleston, South Carolina; Jim Martin, *It Came in the Mail*, reprinted by permission, *Compost in My Shoe* Blog, Charleston, South Carolina; Myra Yeatts, *Everybody's a Critic*, reprinted by permission, moonShine Review, Charlotte, North Carolina.

Cover Illustration: *Tim Mitoma*

Production and Design: *Cathleen O'Brien*

Edited by: *Cheryl Armstrong, Mary Brent Cantarutti, Kate Crawford, Linda Watanabe McFerrin, Martha Dabbs Greenway, Gail Strickland, Julie Thompson, Ann Ure, Sarah Wilcox and Anne Woods*

ISBN-13: 978-1482679045

Published 2013 by Southern Sampler Artists Colony Press
San Rafael, California

Printed in the United States of America

For information about The Southern Sampler Artists Colony
visit our website: www.southernsamplerartistscolony.com

A Southern Sampler

A Southern Sampler *is dedicated to*
Anna Elizabeth Watson *and* Jack McCray,
two rare beings who inspired us to celebrate life,
community, and creative expression. It's their
spirit that draws us back to Charleston,
a beloved place like no other.

The Southern Sampler Artists Colony is a
creative, bi-coastal community woven in belonging.
Together, we discover the magic of words, colors,
images, and notes set to a lazy Lowcountry beat.

A Southern Sampler is our story—a story to be
shared and embellished in time.

Mary Brent Cantarutti and Martha Greenway
California and South Carolina

Place and People

Spirit and Light

Spirit and Light

History and Art

Food and Sustenance

Acknowledgements

Writers Artists Chefs

About the Contributers

There is no value in life except what you

choose to place upon it and no happiness

in any place except what you bring to it yourself.

—Henry David Thoreau

Place
&
People

Southern Exposure: On the Palmetto Trail

Linda Watanabe McFerrin

The size of the snake had grown, in the telling, from the length and breadth of my friend Martha's arm, to the far more dramatic dimensions of her muscular cousin Dickie's. I was at a gathering of the Dabbs clan at one of the old family properties by the Crossroads just east of Black River Swamp in the County of Sumter, South Carolina. Martha and I had been hiking along on the High Hills of Santee Passage of the Palmetto Trail when the large green-brown serpent slithered across our paths and disappeared into the waters of Old Levi Mill Lake. Martha was disturbed; I was ecstatic. I let out a gleeful shriek.

The South is intriguing territory. Home of the blues, gumbos, gators, haunts, hollers, swamps and all their quirky inhabitants, it's also been the stomping grounds of some of my favorite writers—William Faulkner, Flannery O'Connor, Harper Lee, Erskine Caldwell, Alice Walker, even Edgar Allan Poe—sensual, steamy and sometimes scary as hell. As a girl I longed to explore it. As an adult I did, eventually capsizing my canoe and falling into the murky waters of the Okefenokee Swamp. So when southern friends Mary Brent and Martha suggested a visit and Martha mentioned the 425-plus-mile Palmetto Trail, I found the prospect exciting. It wasn't long before I found myself just north of Charleston, South Carolina, heading up US Highway 17 towards Awendaw, the Francis Marion National Forest, Cape Romain National Wildlife Refuge and the point at which the Palmetto Trail hits the sea.

The Palmetto Trail is really not one trail at all. Cobbled together from only a few of the myriad footpaths that fret the state, it is a nearly continuous passageway that stretches from Oconee State Park in the mountainous upstate region to Buck Hall, its low country terminus. A federally designated Millennium Legacy Trail and one of only thirteen cross-state trails in the nation, it crawls down pinnacles, across gorges and swamps, along riverbanks and through forests, traversing some of the most spectacular terrain in the country.

The weather was hot when I emerged from my car at Buck Hall Planta-tion, the cicadas so loud they sounded like buzz saws blazing away in the blistering sunshine. At this watery end of the Palmetto Trail it's an easy jaunt along salt marsh and through verdant maritime forest. Tides creep in here to surround and feed the swamp grass then gently recede. Egrets, cranes, herons and pelicans swoop to graceful landings. Thousands upon thousands of mar-ble-sized fiddler crabs scuttle about in the sands. Young longleaf and loblolly pines sway in the occasional breeze. Fan-like palmettos (South Carolina's state tree) and ancient live oaks, among the only remnants of a venerable generation that managed to weather Hurricane Hugo, offer much welcome shade.

Awendaw Passage connects to the rest of the Palmetto Trail not far from this point via the Swamp Fox Passage, officially the next leg of the journey. A 42-mile forest trek across pinelands and wetlands, over boardwalks and bridg-es and along the defunct railbeds of old logging trams, it ends at Lake Moultrie in Berkeley County at the western edge of the forest. With days rather than weeks to spend on the trail, I opted to take Highway 45 through the wood-lands and I was glad I did. No sooner had I turned inland and into the forest than it started to rain, sprinkling at first as I experimented hastily with my rental car lights and windshield wipers. It was storm season in South Carolina and reminders of the hurricanes that ravage the coast were everywhere. The rain began to hammer away at the car, sluicing off the windows in sheets. Lightening flashed down in long, jagged forks that ended somewhere in the trees around me or on the road up ahead. Jamestown, St. Stephen, Manning— the journey to Martha's was tumultuous and beautiful, and I was genuinely relieved when I finally met her at the far side of Black River Swamp and we turned up the long, narrow drive to her home, the dogs bounding alongside the cars in boisterous greeting.

The weather was clear and warm the next day when Martha and I set out for the High Hills of Santee Passage, the highway bordered by neat little churches and plantation-style homes astoundingly picturesque. We stopped at a roadside shop to pick up a light lunch and picnicked at the trailhead at Poinsett State Park right next to the small lake in which Martha swam as a child. The land is a bit hilly along this 14-mile stretch of the trail, but it is still easy walking. It's also spectacular with wildlife. The sun worked like a powerful soporific, tiring us quickly.

The cicadas droned softly around us like hypnotic, non-stop, battery-powered maracas. Mosquitoes circled hopefully, looking for a break in our prophylactic curtains of repellent. I had been warned that I should be on the lookout for water moccasins on this part of the trail, that the ticks in Sumter County had been known to carry Lyme disease. But I wasn't thinking about any of this, so entranced was I with the green of the water and the ascent and descent of the trail. That's when the elegant green-brown ophidian slithered across our path. A ranger told us later it was very likely a rat snake, and the nearby wood duck nest suggested that this might be the case as these snakes like eggs for breakfast, but it could just as easily have been a somewhat more poisonous reptile. No matter; it didn't bite, which is more than I can say for the tick I brought back to the house.

"Look at this, Martha," I said, pointing to a brand new freckle.

"My Lord, it's a tick," said Martha, deftly plucking it away.

That night Martha and I had dinner with Dickie again, and as we listened to his wild tales of motorcycle adventures in the American outback and stories of the ghosts that share his enormous southern mansion, I was reminded once more why I love the South and its residents.

I'm told the Palmetto Trail becomes much more rigorous as it heads up into the high country, a place of 60-foot waterfalls and 1000-foot ascents, a place to visit when my ankle is stronger and I have a lot more time. One Southern friend said, "Fine trail like that, you can't do it all at once. You have to take it slow." Wise words. I'll be back. The hike isn't over. In fact it's only begun.

The Storm

The storm would have killed my Aunt Elizabeth
   If she were not already dead.
Lain beneath the ground at old Brick Church,
   One life for God's great order already searched.

It would have killed her tree by tree by tree—
   The toppled pines, the uprooted oaks,
The smaller ones like next of kin
   Crushed and tangled by the storm's great wind.

But, had she been here to awaken on that dreadful dawn
   To see the destruction in her woods and lawn,
She would have spared no time for coffee or tea,
   No time for pity or to say, "Poor me."

Donning her work clothes, her hand saw, the shears,
   She'd waste not a second; not afraid of her fears.
"God's order needs help," she'd say out loud.
   "In no time at all, He will again be proud."

Yes, were she not already dead, she would be now.
   If not by the shock of this unplanned chaos,
Then by her sheer determination to set things right,
   To restore the order destroyed that night.

The storm would have killed my Aunt Elizabeth
   If she were not already dead.

—*Martha Dabbs Greenway*

Sundown in Sparkleberry Swamp

Curled around a cypress limb on a sunlit day

the cottonmouth holds, harmless,

like a kitten on a windowsill.

She basks in the warmth,

lazy and innocuous,

above suspicion.

At sunset she stretches to

begin the calculated climb.

Slithering up the knotted trunk

to the nest atop,

its twigs feathered

with the down of osprey,

conforming to ivory orbs

coddling softly beating hearts.

Satiated from her long afternoon nap,

the cottonmouth slowly encircles the largest

unprotected infant like a delicacy.

Nudging with her nose, teasing with her tongue,

she nibbles at the casing before

swallowing the egg whole.

—*Ann Kathleen Ure*

Annabel and Edgar

Annabel sighed again last night
in a dream within a dream,
as she kissed Edgar and held him tight
while wild winds blew extreme.

Her raven hair snaked to her waist,
her eyes laughed like the sun;
she held him close in deep embrace.
His heart she surely won.

She wasn't sick, his Annabel Lee,
and never was taken away
nor placed in a sepulcher; you see,
she was off on holiday.

But Edgar in his black topcoat,
whose calling card was fear,
had to kill off his sweet Annabel
in an ode to his love dear

to save her from the angels of death
or so he heard it said …
that winds blown from their jealous breath
would sadly find her dead.

With blackened ink he penned his verse
of his lovely condemned bride,
to make her sick and getting worse,
to keep her by his side.

His poetry filled and chilled the night
'round her kingdom by the sea,
until the face in the pale moonlight
was the ghost of Annabel Lee.

Now if you are of confused mind
about what happened in this dream,
remember that in gothic rhymes
nothing's ever as it seems.

I've heard that Poe can still be found
at the end of Sullivan's Isle,
not alone or beneath the sandy ground
but with Annabel and a smile.

—Marianne Betterly

Photo: Marriane Betterly

The Wisdom of Pearl

Paula Tevis

Pearl Fryar, the artist and craftsman behind Bishopville, South Carolina's major tourist attraction, did not teach himself topiary nor create his extraordinary garden with the intention of imparting a lesson or enticing the world to this small Southern town. His initial goal was as ordinary as can be: Pearl had something to prove to the neighbors. So, he foraged what he could to transform a three-acre former cornfield into something eye-catching, and within a few years of rescuing the lame and the halt of the plant world, the Bishopville Iris Garden Club awarded him Yard of the Month. His objective was realized. He could retire the hedge clippers. But by this time, Pearl had developed a passion and a dream. It was no longer about keeping up the property; it was now about nurturing a message of love, peace and goodwill, literally carved into the landscape.

That's one lesson big enough to compete with Pearl's massive Cypress trees, but it's not what took root in me after a spring visit to his garden. Now, as I stare out my window onto snow-covered tree limbs and red brick, the constant swoosh of buses and cars the background to my thoughts, the word "patience" insistently comes to mind. How patient Pearl was, and is, to coax life and shape from spindly twigs. How much patience it takes to nurture the plants, to wait for growth, to adapt your ideas to the form developing in front of you, to repeatedly trim the shrubs and trees, no matter the weather or how tired you might feel. To have the patience to wait and see what happens next, rather than attempt to force an outcome.

It's wisdom as useful, adaptable and, I'll dare say, as beautiful as any of Pearl's topiary, but portable, fortunately. Plus, it doesn't require water to grow. Just patience.

Balanced on a dull rock

in the sparkling sand

a Magpie

— *Cathleen O'Brien*
(inspired by Basho)

Nell and Gene

Brenda Bevan Remmes

There are people you love most of the time and those whom you adore all of the time. But then there is a rare circle of characters who are so charming, so original, so unforgettable that you not only enjoy them in advance but continue to laugh with absolute affection, even after they're gone. That was my Uncle Gene and Aunt Nell.

He was a military man, who raised four boys in regimented fashion; she, the daughter of a Methodist minister, partial to varying shades of red hair and long tight skirts. When the boys had all left home she had an epiphany that her life should be more pink. What followed was a complete renovation of their house and wardrobes. Everything became pink. I say this not as whimsical touches of table cloths and dishes. I literally mean rugs, curtains, furniture, all bathroom accessories and clothes, from underwear outward. I can't attest to the fact that Uncle Gene's underwear was pink, but knowing Aunt Nell if I had to bet, I'd give her the upper hand. Like an old war house, he took orders well and he, like everyone else, adored her.

A second epiphany she'd had when the boys left home was that it was no longer necessary to cook. They ate out every meal, dressed in coordinated pink outfits. Breakfast every morning was at Bojangles, then the afternoon and evening meals varied depending on the day of the week. My husband and I always joined them on Friday nights at The Compass, a local fish place. To watch them enter a room was worth the price of the meal. They had become regulars at their favorite restaurants and many people knew them. But even those who didn't would stop and look up when the doors opened and they entered: bright red hair, large pink sunglasses and a tremendous rose cloth flower always pinned to her bodice. Her arm was slipped into the hook of his elbow. He would have a pink shirt with matching socks and a red or purple tie. His pants were sometimes white, in the winter more often black. Heads turned and the room would become quiet as they made their way arm in arm across the floor. She had a bad hip and limped. He was bent with age and shuffled. But they shared smiles with everyone and even those who didn't know them would wave as if they were the Duke and Duchess of Earl.

Sadly, Nell died in 2005. Uncle Gene's health began to decline immediately. Family and friends tried to keep him on his regular outings for lunch and dinner. When he stopped wearing his pink shirts we should have known immediately. We had talked him into joining us at the Compass one Friday night and his son agreed to drive him over. When he came in, his head was bent, his skin pallid. "How you doin', Uncle Gene," I asked as we helped him into a chair.

"Dubious," he said.

My mother sat down across from him and took his hands in hers. "You don't look like you feel too well," she said. He didn't respond, but shortly he appeared to doze off and you could hear the slight murmur of a soft snore.

"His hands are cold," mother said.

"All the time, any more," his son, Rees, said, "they stay cold."

"Shall we order for him?"

"Go ahead. He'll wake back up when the food gets here."

As if nothing were different we chatted away, ourselves and three other cousins: reviewed the week's happenings, caught up on the doings of a few relatives. When the food arrived, Rees was unable to rouse his father.

"Perhaps we should get them to pack up everything and we'll take it back to his house. He might want to lie down," I said. The waitress removed the plates to accommodate us.

"Daddy," Rees said. "Daddy, we're going to take you home. I'm going to pull the car around and we'll eat at home instead."

Gene did not answer, his head still bowed. Rees gave his father a good shake and pulled his head back. Once I saw the deep blue tinges of his lips and his eyes rolled back into the sockets, I knew at once he was dead.

"Uncle Gene's dead, I do believe," I finally said out loud.

"Oh no, not here in this place. Not now," my mother said, horrified.

No one said a word. Rees let his father's head rest back on the table and we all sat motionless for a moment while the waitress returned our food all bagged up in Styrofoam and ready to go. "Anything else?" she asked in a cheery voice.

"Nothing at the moment," I said.

Finally Rees broke the silence. "How are we going to get him out of here?"

Another cousin piped up. "You get him under one arm and I'll get him under the other. I think we could do it."

"A wheel chair would be easier. See anyone with a wheel chair we could borrow?" Mother said.

We took a gander around the crowded restaurant. All the tables were filed. A line twenty-five people deep stood in the doorway of the entrance. It was going to be tough to fool this crowd, but such a shame to ruin everyone's dinner by having someone die in the middle of it.

"We could call the rescue squad," Rees said.

"They make such a scene," Mother said.

I agreed. "They'll hurl him to the floor, rip open his shirt, stuff a tube down his throat. Nasty stuff. It'll all look nasty."

"Would definitely mess up everyone's dinner," a cousin added with raised eyebrows.

"Let's go for trying to carry him out," Rees said.

Almost as the decision was made, sirens wailed in the background. Four men with stretchers came hurdling past the patrons at the door to the complete surprise of the hostess. As we knew they would, they hurled Uncle Gene to the floor, tore open his shirt and immediately began CPR. Everything in the restaurant stopped.

"Who called them?" I said in disgust as I looked up at the front door and saw my husband shrug his shoulders and raise his cell phone. I should have known. He's from Iowa; so practical, so logical about his approach to life and death. I made my way through the crowd. "Why did you do that?"

"Maybe he wasn't dead," he said. "It seemed like the thing to do."

Murmurs of "he's dead," began rippling through the restaurant as the rescue guys loaded the body on the stretcher and moved to the ambulance. I gave him my best "I-told-you-so" glare and headed to get mother.

"I think we could have handled that better," Mother said. "It didn't have to be such an event."

My cousins were handling the bill and packing up the boxes of food as we made our way to the door. "We'll follow the ambulance to the hospital," I suggested.

She nodded her head in agreement as tears began to appear. "I'm just so sorry this didn't happen at the Country Club instead. We could have classed it up a bit for him. Don't you think?"

Waves lap on the shore
A gray heron stands sentry
Being coos…whispers

—*Mary Brent Cantarutti*

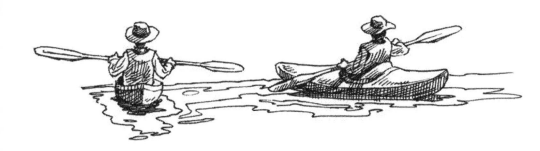

Wambaw Creek meets the South Santee River

Photo: Kathy China

Photo: Ursula Bendixen

Boneyard Beach • Bull's Island

Photo: Sarah Wilcox

St. Michael's Church Steeple

Ships slip out to sea
It's a beach like no other
Breathing in the night

Tides bring gifts to shore
Jellies glisten in the sun
Deliverance waits

—*Mary Brent Cantarutti*

A Crab Story

Anton DuMars

Upon landing onto Morris Island, my tour group quickly crossed the bow, amphibious assault-style. Armed with bucket and plastic bags, each set out on their own beach reconnaissance mission away from the *Tideline*. Now alone on the boat, I peered into the makeshift five-gallon bucket aquarium. There I found a hermit crab, spilling out of its undersized mobile home, a moon snail shell. A month later, driving down I-95 to Aunt Aida's surprise birthday party in Auburndale, Florida, I remember that hermit crab in the bucket.

It was 1967. My mother cobbled together a family summer trip from Fresno, California to Greenwood, Florida, her childhood home. Five kids, age three to thirteen, and a single Mother, traveled by train across the country to New Orleans. For three days, I lived in perpetual wonderment. I explored the entire train from one end to the other. I viewed mountains from the dome car, ate exotic train food in the diner car, and met all sorts of new people. On my eighth birthday, I looked out the window to see my name on the water tower as we passed through Anton, Texas. Mom rented a car in New Orleans and drove us to Mobile. There, Mom's sister, Aida, met us and drove through the night the final four hours to the one-stoplight town of Greenwood, Florida.

Greenwood represents one of several small towns dotting the Florida panhandle. Two Egg lies two miles south, Marianna eight miles west, and Bascom and Malone five miles approximately east. From Aunt Aida's car window, the sun cast its first light on the landscape. An unfamiliar musty dampness filled my nostrils. Unlike the dry San Joaquin Valley, lush greenery crowded both sides of the rural highway. We passed sinkholes, springs, and small swampy rivers.

Soon we arrived at my mother's childhood home, a somewhat run-down two-story, antebellum tin-roof farmhouse, surrounded by huge oaks and pecan trees. Uncle Charles, shirtless, met us from a back room as we entered the house. Thirty minutes later, I found myself on a side porch, shirtless, shelling field peas and butter beans with cousins I'd never met. Shirtless, I remained the rest of the summer.

Later that summer, we visited Aunt Aida and Uncle Dean, and my cousins Jeff and Laurie in St. Petersburg. While there, I learned about salty gulf water, stinging eyes, and new pets like hermit crabs. Hermit crabs don't do well away from the ocean. My new pet crab made the trip back to Greenwood, but gave up the ghost a few days later.

Arriving back to the boat from the beach on Morris Island, my six and eight-year-old guests promptly checked on their hermit crab pet in the bucket. Remembering my childhood experience, I suggested we let it go, back into the salt marsh to rejoin friends. On the way to the marina, we made a special side trip into Mud Bar Creek and set the crab free.

My Mother Among the Dancers

James McBride Dabbs

I have returned from a day's hunting in the woods, and am sitting down to the pumpkin pie she has saved for me. The scene is like herself: she was warm and fruitful, an autumn woman.

One scene from this autumn shines in my memory. It was just before sunrise, on the first day of school, in September. Mother had risen early to make coffee for my brother and me before we did the milking. As we stood on the eastern piazza in the fresh September dawn drinking our coffee with Mother standing beside us, the sky grew rosy beyond the quiet pines. I don't remember anything that was said. I'm sure very little was, for we were a silent family, especially before breakfast; but I realize now that the situation expressed a significant mood. Mother was sending us out to the simple job of milking as though to an adventure. She had dignified the task by her presence and attention; she had made it, however faintly, a personal matter. She was a lady and it was dawn, and there was work to do. I sometimes wonder whether this picture is not the key to my life, the clue to all I've done.

For there was something—oh, so faint—of dawn in the lady, something of the lady in the dawn. There was a kind of tenderness in both, and both were silent. They did not need to speak; they were important without words. In my thirteenth year the lady died; she was made one with nature; and the rest is silence. Perhaps the silence of her death has flowed backward to deepen the silence of her life. I don't know. I feel sure, however, that for twelve years she was at the heart of my life, and she lives in my memory in silence. She was the human counterpart and core of the surrounding silence of nature: the vital silence of dawn, the quiet silence of sundown, the strange silence of the stars. About one silence, and within another, and driven by something of my father's strenuous will, my life followed its orbit. Considering that cosmic air, I am not surprised that I should sometimes wonder what life is: the action or the rest, the sound or the silence.

So were my early years blessed by the presence of a mother who expressed some natural mystery in her step, and in her life some friendliness with far, beneficent powers.

But in the beginning at least that was only the rippling into space of the human affection that she lavished about her, which had been distilled within her by happy girlhood scenes. I remember again her early home, the Winter House, with its boxwood garden, long since gone. I don't know why it went, nor just when. It stood far back from the house, and was surrounded by a latticed fence and entered through a latticed gate. Just inside the gate, beneath a rose arbor to the left, there was a bed of violets; you knelt upon the brick wall to pick them. Their cool, sweetness was the sweetness of the house, and the formality of the boxwood was its formality. Where the garden was there is a field now; the garden may never be there again. But I have never forgotten its sweet formality, its hint of rich life I scarcely remember. Once—only once—I saw the house ablaze with light and my mother among the dancers.

Only once, too, do I remember my father among the ax-men. But pondering these pictures now, I think they tell my story. Somewhat like my father, I have tried to cut my way through the world; somewhat like my mother, I have swayed to the pressure of the moment. I have struggled with a god who, in my father's spirit, laid down impossible demands; I have also found myself momentarily in the drawing room of the universe, whose supernal light my mother had received from and given to the dawn. The spirit of these two opposing pictures has shaped my life.

Excerpt from The Road Home, *published in 1960.*

To My Husband, the Artist

For you the colors of crushed jewels

For me, the artistry of words.

So Beauty is the bond that binds us

In Love as boundless as the flight of birds.

—*Elizabeth Dabbs Thompson*

Chopping Cotton

Cheryl Armstrong

The summer I turned eleven, my mother sent my little brother Gib and me to Grammy's farm while she stayed in California to sort things out with my daddy. When she got to Oklahoma in August, I was the last in line to hug her and feel her skinny bones. Gib was crying, he was so happy. He showed her his pet horned toad, Elvis.

On the front porch that evening the family asked about daddy. "He's struggling, Momma," my mother said. "His friends call him 'Major'." He's holding on to that. He can't figure out what he's good at."

"He's good at drinking," Uncle Pete said.

"Liquor kills the spirit," Granddaddy said.

I put Elvis in his box on the porch and headed off to bed without saying goodnight. I was still awake when my mother came in later with Gib. She let him climb in her bed, and even though it was a warm night, wrapped her arm around him. I wished I had something to hold onto.

At breakfast the next morning, Granddaddy said grace. "Thank you Lord, for this fine food and this family that is gathered together to partake. Thank you for bringing Adelia safely to us from California. Thank you for this fine food. We are grateful to be eating it in your presence."

Grammy made the usual breakfast. Duke and Don, my mother's youngest brothers, and Granddaddy, served themselves eggs, bacon and biscuits, pouring syrup over everything. Granddaddy drank coffee and my uncles drank warm milk with a dash of coffee and four spoons of sugar. Momma nibbled at a little bit of biscuit and eggs. I ate ham with syrup. Grammy stood by the stove. She never did sit down with us for meals, not even supper.

After Granddaddy and the boys went off to start their day, my mother and I were still at the table and she nudged my leg with her bare foot and said, "Let's get started."

"What are you two girls up to?" asked Grammy.

"We're going to chop cotton."

"Oh Adelia, you don't need to do that. Your daddy will get your brothers to do it."

"I do need to do it, Momma. It's part of the farm experience. And I want company." She smiled at me.

We put on worn flannel men's shirts, so thin they were light and cool, and pairs of Don's old jeans that we only had to roll up a little. "That's to keep the scratches down," my mother said. She grabbed a couple of straw hats from the cooking shed and a couple of hoes and pairs of work gloves from the tool shed.

"You girls want a ride?" Don asked, starting up the Ford tractor, on his way to the peanut field. I was embarrassed at how I looked.

"No, we're fine, Donald," my mother said. "It's not that far."

Grammy brought us a jar of lemon water and a jar of pickle juice water. "Don't you go letting her get heat stroke now, Adelia."

"Don't worry, Momma, we'll be just fine."

We put on our hats, slung the hoes over our shoulders, and each carried a jar. I followed Momma to the cotton field, fixing my eyes on her footprints in the dust. I was already sweaty under my armpits.

When we got to the first row, she said, "Looks like someone has been chopping cotton already."

"Duke."

"What did he do?" she asked.

"Said some swear words."

"OK we'll do these two rows. You do this one and I'll do that one." She grabbed my jar and set them both on the ground partway down her row. "That's where we'll take a little break, help us measure our progress. Now chopping cotton isn't chopping cotton. You don't chop the cotton. You chop what isn't the cotton." She scraped at the sprouts of grass and weeds around the base of the first cotton plant. I did the same for mine.

"Daddy and the boys can turn over the furrows between the rows, but they can't get right up to the plants and in between them," she went on. "That's where we help out."

I figured out how to tilt the hoe so that the sharp point gouged the weed out of the earth.

"Don't get too close to the stalk," my mother warned.

If there was a plant right up against the stalk, I'd reach down with my fingers to pull it out. It was slow work. If my mother got too far ahead of me, she'd cross over to my row and work her way back.

"You're doing a good job there, Joycie," she said. "You're doin' real good."

I got thirsty. I rubbed at the sweat on my face with my sleeve. Stickers scraped against my skin and got in the neck of my shirt.

"You know," she said, "I feel I've been chopping cotton all my life. Seeing Margaret's little baby Mark reminds me of something from when I was about your age."

My hands were hurting. Even with gloves on I could feel blisters forming.

"I was a little bit older than you and Momma was heavy with Gwen. She left Margaret and Charlotte in charge of Lodema, Leon and Darwin. They were to stay near the house and sort pinto beans, rake the chicken yard and stay out of trouble."

Now my arms ached, too. I glanced on ahead at the water jars.

"I could tell by Momma's huffing that she was ready to deliver that baby. 'Momma,' I said, 'we got to go in to the house. We got to send for Mrs. Taylor.' Mrs. Taylor was the midwife and she lived on down the road. 'Not yet,' she kept saying, chopping and chopping. I couldn't hardly do a good job what for worrying about her. I thought she'd have that baby right here in the field."

My mother stopped chopping and pulled a hankie out of her back pocket and wiped her face. She pulled another out and handed it to me. It was crocheted all around in pink thread.

"Finally I just sort of pushed Momma all the way back to the house. She stopped every once in a while to bend over and breathe. 'Oh, my,' she'd say, 'oh, my.' I was so scared that baby'd be born right there in the cotton field or the chicken yard. Luckily, Daddy saw us going in and met us at the back door. He put Momma in the truck and Gwen was born not five minutes after they got to Mrs. Taylor's house. That's how Gwen got her name. Mrs. Taylor's Christian name was Gwendolyn."

I was so glad when we got to the water jars.

"Sip slow, sweetie," my mother told me. "You'll get a tummy ache."

The lemon water was lightly sweetened.

"I prefer pickle juice water," Momma said. "I always did have a salt tooth."

We did one row each that first morning. Actually, my mother did her row and a large part of mine. As we made our way back down the rows toward the house, I saw the weeds and baby grass we had chopped were already withered and drying in the sun. I had taken my hat off half way down the row and made the hankie into a kind of crown on my brow. My arms, neck and ankles itched from the burrs and pieces of grass.

We took an outdoor shower to get the dust off and I didn't care who might try to peek over the stall and see me. My mother's hipbones stuck out; she was that skinny.

"You're developing a little figure, Joycie," she said. I blushed. "And a tummy."

"Oh, that felt good," she said when we sat at the kitchen table wearing only Granddaddy's old t-shirts and our underwear, our bare feet on the cool linoleum. "It's just too hot for clothes." We drank iced tea and I could barely lift the glass to my lips, it felt so heavy.

"We'll do two more rows tomorrow," she said. "And before you know it, we'll be as strong as Duke and Don."

That night I lay down right after dinner in my clothes, fell sound asleep and didn't wake up until after the sun rose. I dreamed of bubbles and dry bones.

Excerpt from Geronimo, *a work in progress.*

Photo: Cheryl Armstrong

Ravenel Bridge

There was an old gal at the crossroads

She lived in a house full of horned toads

She'd see them at night; 'bout croaked at the sight

And the toads peed on all the floor boards

—*Martha Dabbs Greenway*

Tide Country

Anton DuMars

Driving home across the James Island connector from Charleston, still smarting from my second parking ticket in less than a week, I realize my current "parking plan" needs updating. Parking tickets don't fit well into a geology adjunct's budget. Headlights stab the darkness, lighting up two lanes channeled between parallel concrete barriers. My present thoughts don't wander far beyond a hot dinner and a cold beer waiting for me on Folly Beach. Car windows down on a welcoming cool night, I smell the pungent, sulfury scent of a multi-species ecosystem thriving just beyond visibility. I'm reminded of my preferred *other* job, my alter ego as an eco-tour guide in the very marshes I now smell.

Recently, on a tour, a dolphin broke the surface and took a breath just in front of the bow, startling a young Indian couple. He came from New Delhi and she from Kholkata. First becoming acquainted as neighbors and PhD students attending the University of North Carolina, Chapel Hill, they now shared a romantic get-a-way to Folly Beach. Neither had met the other's parents. Fifty miles south of Kholkata, the Brahma Putra and the Ganges rivers meets the Bay of Bengal, forming the Sundarbans, a.k.a. the "tide country". Here Bengal tigers patrol the islands, while large crocodiles snatch unwary fishermen from boats. She from Kolkata leaned over the side, searching the surface to sight her first wild dolphin. Fortunately for her, our salt marshes and hammocks harmlessly invite the curious in for a closer look.

The U.S. east coast, as do most shorelines, experiences two tidal cycles per day. This is known as a semi-diurnal tidal regime. From dead low to dead high tide, Folly Beach's sea level rises vertically just less than 6 feet (on average) in 6 hours 13 minutes, moving the tidal cycle ahead approximately 51 minutes each day. The moon and, to a lesser degree, the sun literally pull an ellipsoid-shaped bulge of ocean around the earth, flooding and draining our marshes twice daily through an endless capillary-like network of tidal creeks.

Tidal variation produces distinct vertical ecological zones. An extreme low tide exposes red beard sponges and sea whip corals. Bivalves, such as oysters and clams, occupy creek banks between average low and high water, while *Spartina alterniflora* (marsh grass) dominates mean high tide elevation. Constantly changing water levels force marsh animals to change feeding tactics with the tides. As tidal waters flood over the top of them, oysters open up and resume filter feeding. Chicken-like oyster catchers take advantage and move in for their namesake meal. At high tide, shrimp and fish find refuge among flooded marsh grass. Flooded marshes also invite red drum to swim onto tidal flats in search of blue crabs. At low tide, with the marsh grass drained and hiding places eliminated, prey becomes more vulnerable. Also at low tide, dolphins engage in strand feeding, coordinating to school mullet right out of the water onto mud banks. With my hydrophone, I recorded a dolphin giving the "charge" signal just before a small pod simultaneously stormed the sandbar at Morris Island. This to me was the marine equivalent of capturing "Big Foot" on film.

Arriving home just after 9pm, dogs and wife greet me. Food and cold beer consumed, I relax into my comfort zone on Folly Beach, realizing I'm the luckiest man alive. For with tomorrow, the adventure continues.

Photo: Anne Woods

Where Are They Now

Where are they now,
The flowers that yesterday
So gaily gave their sweetness
To the air?
Vanished in time,
In space perhaps they still
Sweeten eternal summer
With some perfume rare.

—Sophie McBride Dabbs

Photo: Cathleen O'Brien

The Dusty Grande Dame of Charleston

Unity Barry

Musty mansions inhabited by former slave owners' descendants, faded glory, damp decomposition—that was the gray vision I once held of the South. Like Hollywood's black and white depictions of Tennessee Williams' work and books by other Southern Gothic novelists like William Faulkner and Flannery O'Connor, I expected Charleston, South Carolina to fit neatly into my prejudices.

Mary Brent Cantarutti and Martha Greenway, the two organizers of the Southern Sampler Artists Colony, opened my eyes to a beautiful city that proved me wrong. My biases were washed away when I saw the tide of cultural and urban restoration that marks this gracious metropolis. Sophisticated Charlestonians are proud of the beauty and heritage that mark the area. Top chefs use a mélange of world class ingredients to honor traditional foods of the region. Downtown still retains the narrow streets of the early seventeen hundreds. No misguided renewal efforts scar the cityscape with twentieth century mediocrity. Gardens flourish in the muggy climate, spilling out over brick walls and through wrought iron fences. Galleries and museums overflow with quality crafts and fine art. The Gullah culture of African slaves is honored with living examples of language, crafts and foods like jambalaya and gumbo. The Charleston Jazz Initiative actively works to preserve the stories and music of the numerous greats like Dizzy Gillespie who got their start there.

A reverence for history pervades the city, so it is no surprise that numerous mansions are preserved in their finest splendor. The ugly scar of slavery has not been masked, however. The old slave market is a museum and reminder how early Charlestonians used human misery to become one of the richest cities on the North American continent.

The startling exception to the restored antebellum exuberance that flourishes there is the Aiken-Rhett House, which echoed my former jaundiced vision of the South. Built in 1820 it is a time capsule of an "urban plantation."

The stables, kitchens, laundry and slave quarters now feature damaged walls and ceilings, but otherwise remain just as they would have been nearly 200 years ago. Dusty tools and kitchenware are left as if vacating occupants forgot to return for the last load of belongings. The descendants of Gov. William Aiken, Jr. lived there for 150 years, doing little to change it except to add electricity and heat to some of the rooms. Because of that, it was donated virtually unaltered since 1858. After the turn of the twentieth century, the family chose to close off many of the rooms, hermetically freezing the past *in situ*. Much of the original furniture and art works are still in their same places in the home, waiting to be cleaned and polished. In many ways the house reminded me of Miss Havisham's dining room in *Great Expectations*. While there is no rotting food or elegant wedding tableware, there is the same sense of dusty disintegration. The Historic Charleston Foundation, the mansion's current owners, took the unusual approach of preserving it rather than returning it to its full pre Civil War grandeur. The layers of wallpaper have been left to peel, revealing intense color and patterns. Faded paint covers plaster layers of the service areas and slave quarters.

As we walked through the property, following the self-guided tour's audio player, I couldn't help but imagine two separate visions of the home's past. One picture was of classic Southern belles dressed in hoop skirts and flirting behind rapidly beating fans. Candlelight reflected in shining gilt-framed mirrors while shadowy help kept silent counsel as they served their masters. The second play of my mind's theater was set on the stage as it existed before me— dark to aid preservation, dust infrequently disturbed once the army of cleaners and caretakers vanished, walls moldy from humidity and frequent storms. The actors would be generations of heirs who lost their family's staggering income with the surrender at Appomattox Courthouse. With only pride and a storied past, they hunkered down in ever decreasing circumstances, slowly drawing into smaller quarters as the needs of the mansion became too much.

Some claim the house is haunted. Many attest to sightings of people in period dress. Others report hearing unaccounted for footsteps. It's easy to understand why. Whether these experiences are the workings of people who, like me, are transported to another realm by the atmosphere of the place, or who have truly bumped into restless spirits—it doesn't matter. It is enough that Aiken-Rhett house exists, an antique grande dame struggling to hold her own as the last musty mansion of Charleston.

Purple Martins

Mary Brent Cantarutti

The purple martins were lined up on the overhead wires, chirping madly, when they returned to the cabin. They had been standing sentinel while Lou and Charlie were away on vacation. Now the birds welcomed them home joyfully. It wasn't the first time Charlie had been comforted by the sight and sound of the purple martins. Glancing up at the evenly spaced gourds hanging from crossbars attached to a hinged metal pole, he was reminded of a day long ago, watching as his grandfather and father sunk the tall pole into the ground. In his mind, he could hear Grandfather DuBose's confident voice. "The purple martins are going to be our friends, Charlie. They'll keep the mosquito population down in the summer. Just you wait and see."

In those days Charlie was always waiting for something: waiting to grow up; to be recognized; to be strong enough to help his grandfather and father dig a giant hole in the hard earth and hoist the ungainly metal pole skyward, securing it with globs of gooey cement. But he never felt lonely when it came to waiting for the purple martins. Charlie waited with his grandfather, Calvin DuBose, for the bird gourd seeds they planted in the carefully tilled earth to sprout; waited for the tender vines to stretch towards the welcoming sun; waited for the gourds to dry so that he could draw a big cross on each gourd, so that his grandfather, Calvin, could cut around the outside of the cross, creating an entrance for the martins.

Charlie was eight when Calvin died. He waited for his grandfather to come back. The waiting ended when Charlie accompanied his father, Robert DuBose, to Fuller's Hardware store in Clarksville, where they bought plastic bird gourds. Charlie knew then that things change, and that waiting didn't make any difference. But the purple martins, like long-time lovers, returned each spring. Charlie and his father continued to prepare for the arrival of the lively birds whose raven-like feathers glistened metallic purple in the sun. It was in early fall, after the martins had flown south, that they carefully unhinged the tall pole and lowered the crossbars. Together they cleaned the vacated gourds, removing the pine straw, bits of string and twigs collected to build nests, along with downy feathers left by the fledging offspring. It fell to Charlie to hose out each gourd before handing it to his father for drying and applying a sprinkling of powdered sulfite to prevent an infestation of mites. One by one they tied the clean gourds to the metal crossbars, and together raised the bars skyward. Preparing for the return of the purple martins was their way of honoring the past, acknowledging the seasons, and holding close the promise of renewal in the face of loss.

Many years later, in March, shortly after his father's death, Charlie had come to the lake in search of a quiet place to reflect and sift through the shards of grief. Much to his surprise, the purple martin scouts were there, claiming early ownership of the gourds they called home year after year. It seemed that his father had sent them with a message: To everything there is a time, a season. My spirit will always return to DuBose Bay.

Excerpt from her forthcoming book The Bottle Tree.

On Sullivan's Island

for Mary Brent

It was in motion—
fire-bright and cardinal,
quick as spark
and sparklers pirouetting
through the nights
I remember
when the stars tented our
adventures in a carnival
hilarity that swept us
away, breathless as the children
who have blown out all the candles,
whose wish is about
to come true.

—*Linda Watanabe McFerrin*

Photo: Cheryl Armstrong

Ode to us!

Kissed by the sunshine in the morning,

Rattled into submission by the inspiration,

Feeling the music,

Moving to the poetry,

Marveling with Marv,

Draped over Mary Brent's arm walking at sunrise,

Stretching and moving with Kathy until our legs were sore,

Catching the joy of language with Linda,

Praying peacefully with Martha,

Singing from the soul with Kitty and Paula,

Strolling with Sarah,

Reflecting on the porch with Unity …

We marched to the tune of Alphonso Brown.

Rhythms shook our cores with their spirituals.

Loving food made for us by Cathleen

And her joyous laughter,

Jolting to the jazz of Karen Chandler,

Embracing Marlene's stories,

Reveling in Joanna's poetry,

It was a week of love.

Being caressed in the nurturing arms of women,

Carried by the waves to a place of tranquility,

Softly partaking in the sunset,

Women enriching our souls,

Weaving the threads of creation,

Telling our stories that need to be told,

Sharing intimate moments of joy,

We move the earth with our presence.

Partaking in the miracle of birth and creation,

Loving gratitude coursing through our veins,

Lucky, possessed by the Spirit of Charleston,

Dancing at midnight,

Moving to the refrains,

Glorious women, dance naked in the sun.

Speak your truth in loud voices.

Twist and turn along the journey.

Continue with courage

In loving gratitude.

—Cindy Rasicot

We are connected—
purple martins, cardinals—
our island Twitter.

—*Linda Watanabe McFerrin*

There's a lovely old house on Sullivan's
That was leased to a bunch of wild hooligans
They howled at the moon, lay nude on the dunes
And all were jailed by high noon.

—*Martha Dabbs Greenway*

A Southern Boy's Conversion

Red clay hugs

shoes untied

Feeling untried

rise like froth

on the warm cow's milk

Watery eyes

fears buzzing like flys

Emotions erupt

in an ecstasy of

peach fuzz

and

June bugs

—*Billy Vandiver*

Alligator Alley

We were watchful walkers.
We tottered on our tip toes.

An afternoon hike on Bull's Island.

Belonging

Mary Brent Cantarutti

Do y'all ever think about belonging? We Southerners know that belonging is our birthright, like forgiveness tied up for Christmas with a big red bow, but I never gave it a lot of thought until I started stirring the creative pot—Southern style—with writer and artist friends from the San Francisco Bay Area. The first Southern Sampler Artists Colony Writers Workshop in Charleston brought us together. It was 2009. Curiosity might have motivated folks to head south initially, but as for what brings them back year after year, I'll put my money on belonging.

Maybe belonging begins with *hey y'all*, an irresistible drawling invitation to slow down and discover sunrise strolls along the Battery, canopies of live oaks, side porches, rocking chairs, tucked away gardens, steeples galore, the Gullah language, sweetgrass baskets, Lowcountry jazz beats, and culinary wonders rooted in row farming traditions.

Photo: Linda Watanabe McFerrin

The best and most beautiful things in the world

cannot be seen or even touched —

they must be felt with the heart.

—Helen Keller

Spirit & Light

Wholeness: Giving Birth to Fully Conscious ME by Torreah "Cookie" Washington

Wholeness: Giving Birth to Fully Conscious ME

Torreah "Cookie" Washington

I am Woman/ Mother giving birth to myself

I am The Unbearable Lightness of Being, the animus, full of physical power, free, soft, gentle, kind, innocent and caring, self aware, child-like, fully living in the now moment, physically powerful, rooted in the earth.

I am Woman/ Mother giving birth to myself

I am also, the powerful Sacred Dark Feminine, the Sophia Wisdom, the anima, one who is with you in your darkest hour. I have been named "fear incarnate" so I have resisted embracing the darkness of me.... I now embrace this part of myself , and my fear shall become the power to transform destruction and negativity into strength, hope, wisdom and JOY

I am Woman/ Mother a ubiquitous, irrepressible,

life bringing force

I am Woman/ Mother giving birth to myself

A self that is "Wholeness"

I am a golden child that is female and male

Dark and light, Spirit filled yet nature made

full of love both profane and deeply sacred.

I am sitting here on the bank of this river gathering me back to myself. I can see in both directions while moving purposely forward with new potential and power.

Gospel Truth

"Humpback! Humpback!"
the preachers cry.
Yet a soul's not beached
on sex and 'nana pie.

All I know is I never get high
on that old time gospel
"Doublespeak I."

—*Billy Vandiver*

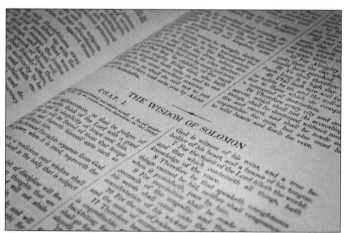

Photo: Anne Woods

Photo: Anne Woods

Curls and Nails

Myra Yeatts

I was getting my roots done at Curls and Nails. Pearl had put the color on, and I was just waiting while she washed somebody two booths over.

Well, I hear this voice from the booth beside me. I don't reckon Polly or her customer even knew I was sitting there. If they did, I don't imagine that they suspected anybody my age could hear as well as I do.

"Well, Priscilla. You sure are looking pink and purty today. You just practically glow."

"Why, thank you. I do feel younger than I have in years. Working seems to agree with me."

"I wouldn't think you'd have to work with the kind of settlement you got. But I'm glad you're enjoying it."

"I don't have to work. I'm just getting out of the house. With the children in college, I needed something to keep me busy."

Now I recognized that snotty voice. She'd got a passel of money off that carousing ex-husband of hers. I glued myself to that conversation like a hair in a biscuit.

"And how do you like plant work?"

"My goodness, Polly, I don't work in the plant. I work in the manager's office."

"Oh, I know that. I was just wondering if you liked working with folks over there. Seems like y'all wouldn't have much in common."

"Oh, you'd be surprised."

"Well now, Ms. Waddell, I do believe you're blushing. I bet you there's a man somewhere in all this."

I listened to all that girlish laughter, and got worried that Pearl would come back to me before they got down to specifics. Polly had a way of sucking the last bit of information out of her customers. I relished my ringside seat, cause Polly don't ever spill nothing her customers tell her. I leaned a little closer to the partition.

"Is it anybody I know?"

"Probably not. He's not from around here."

"Well, who is it? I thought that place had a policy against people that work together dating."

"Polly, as much as I'd like to share this secret with you, I can't. It's complicated, you see."

"He ain't married is he?"

"Well, he's not free yet, but he's working on it."

"Oh my! You better be careful, honey. You don't want to get caught and lose your job over some married man."

"We try to keep our relationship on the QT. I am a few years his senior and, well, you know how it is here."

"Married and younger than you. No wonder you're blushing. Just be careful. Don't be making eyes at him at work. Don't even have lunch with him. People talk and people watch. If you're not careful, your boss will find out."

It got real quiet in there, and for a minute I thought I was going to have to turn up my hearing aid another notch. Then I heard Polly suck in her breath like she does when something gets away with her.

"Oh my goodness gracious! Sweet Jesus! It's your boss ain't it? Come on, Priscilla. You might as well fess up. We've known each other since third grade. You can't hide nothing from me."

"Shhh. Somebody will hear you. Are you going to blow dry my hair or not?"

"Now don't go getting persnickety on me. What's said to me, stays with me. Course it might cost you a bigger tip. Don't look at me like that. You know I'm just yanking your chain."

"Would you please keep quiet. Your excitement is bound to attract attention."

"Okay, okay. How did it all happen?"

"We were working late one night and we started talking. We found that we had so much in common. We have similar tastes in music, and we both love the theater. Our children attend the University of South Carolina together. They aren't in the same social circles, but it gave us pause at how much we have in common."

"Is he good looking or just good?"

"Stop it, Polly! Don't be crude. I truly believe that I've found my soul mate."

"Speaking of soul, I could have sworn that I heard the manager was some black guy from New York."

Wouldn't you know it? That's exactly when my hearing aid took a notion to do that squealing thing it does sometimes. By the time I got it fixed, there won't a sound from next door. That's alright. I heard enough. I love getting my hair fixed.

Truth

Truth

Is relative

Flips, twirls, and settles briefly

Speaks loud and clear, especially when in opposition

Coos late at night when the righteous God sleeps

Is wrapped around the church steeple

Roots for a football team

Tastes like fried food and sweet ice tea

Rocks on the front porch

Cradles the past

Believes nothing will change in the future

Seeks community

Cuts away what doesn't belong

—*Mary Brent Cantarutti*

Release

Upon the yellowed page the black
Notes are clustered like dark stars
That with the mind's renewing light
Become bright wounds from ancient scars.

Obedient to the starry signs
My fingers with their practiced skill
Release the sounds imprisoned there
By the long dead musician's will.

But climbing up the heavenly boughs
In intricate patterns of the past
My soul too swiftly lifts its wings
And strange new sounds are crowding fast;

And though I stare upon dark stars,
I see them not; unseen the page;
Intent upon tumultuous sounds
And rhythms of a newer age;

Unknown chords, strange arpeggios,
The blustering of winter rain,
And broken laws of harmony,
And through it all a wild refrain,

Whose rhythms change, whose tempos leap
Toward some distant starry goal,
Where swift I follow, letting slip
The broken chains that bound my soul.

—*Guy McBride Dabbs*

De Hag

"Hags is human people,
and dey can catch a ole black cat
and boil it and take a bone and hole it in dey mouth."

De Hag exist everywhere,
De Hag slides under doors,
De Hag changes it shape.

De Hag comes at night,
De Hag purloin sleep,
De Hag sits on your body.

De Hag feeds on your breath,
De Hag suck your lungs,
De Hag flies away.

Be sure to sleep with a fork
under your pillow — to keep
De Hag away.

—Cathleen O'Brien

(notes from Linda Ferguson's reading of Eliza Lucas Pinckney's poem "The Hag")

Tides of Sorrow

Last spring the tides of sorrow
Swept across my soul
And all but devoured me
In their turgid depths.
Slowly I raised my head
Above the wave
And drew a breath—

O stabbing pain!
I longed to slip beneath
The cool green wave
And rest beside you.
Relentless life.
Why do you cling to me?
(Or is it I to you?)
Slowly, slowly did the pain recede
From my extremities
Leaving them numb.
Then gathering all his strength
The master marksman
Loosed his dart
And plunged it in my heart.

Comes spring again,

My dearest dear,

In all her beauty

Rivaling your canvases—

And you not here!

O slowly, slowly does the pain depart

Leaving an empty heart.

—*Elizabeth Dabbs Thompson*

Elizabeth by Cathleen O'Brien

Anna Elizabeth Watson

blue ...

the South Carolina flag

those dreamy eyes

the way the world feels

without you

—Linda Watanabe McFerrin

Untitled for Daddy

When we try to see the path before us

The Faux Pas is in our gaze

Eye on the ground a plan to be found

Where each step should quietly lay

We see many roads before us

Some golden, some grim, and some plain

But the key to good sight

Is knowing it's right

Even when you're falling away

—*Anna Elizabeth Watson*

Our Love Song

It's not just our words

Which weave us together

Or our fingers laced softly

Stopping our separation

There is nothing needed to bind us

No commitment or obligation is greater

Than our mere existence

We sing the song of our love with our breath

Pulling each other within to fill and feed

Finding with each breath exchanged

Our limits fade

We are no longer bound to our bodies

The separation of space disappears

And we are free to weave

Long glistening strands of excitement

Thick wet yards of passion

Warm gentle understanding lines

Our lives

A soft lulling symphony

Song of our love.

—Anna Elizabeth Watson

A Proof on Hope

You can not kill every seed in this world

It is not possible to quiet the light

The fire of existence
    will continue to burn
In the moments
    of dampening darkness

The Fire will continue to relight

All that has been will be reborn

        —*Anna Elizabeth Watson*

Continental Checkers

Move with me
On the melody of my mind
Blowing softly thru
The Gullies
Caressing our souls against the hillside

Our Longing

           Blowing Sails

Gliding majesty of Man and Mother
Monuments to Motion.
Memory given to a space moved.
Check

Air & Skin

           And
Ourselves

Blossoms of memory blushing our cheek
Together we rejoice in the pool of memory.
And Ourselves.
Mate.

—*Anna Elizabeth Watson*

Photo: Anne Woods

Ghost Veils

Spanish moss drips
from oak and elm,
hangs like gray veils
on a ghost bride.

Wind moans
through the branches
while they cry.

Some say spirits
live in trees.

I think the moss
mourns young brides
who lost their lives
before their innocence,
like the orange blossom bride
buried in her wedding dress.

The gray moss wraps each tree in a web,
but unlike a victim,
the tree welcomes its invader
and wears the long, tangled threads
as if floating down the aisle,
while Carolina breezes swirl
its ancient silks …
antebellum lace.

—*Marianne Betterly*

Photo: Marianne Betterly

Lowcountry Language

It's a new language,
Here, in the succulent Carolinian air.
We are a bright flock of kayaks
floating down Wambaw Creek,
where gators patrol their territory,
eyes and rough-hilled backs above the water,
letting you know who owns the place.
After all, they
outlasted dinosaurs.

Here vireos come to nest
after feeding in Brazil.
Black swallowtail kites
make a sharp silhouette
against the sky;
the rangers are counting them:
their return
means the salamanders and frogs are back,
those damp, delicate harbingers
of the river's repair.
Wild white Cherokee rose drapes the trees,
and the wax myrtle makes its berries
that colonials melted and boiled for candles.
Their bug-resistant bay-scented leaves
served the native tribes beset with
southern swarms of biting bugs.

A yellow-crowned heron rises
large and windy from the branches

where sits a nest that can survive
hurricanes.
A cardinal flies across a field,
red light racing like rubies
against the green.

The language of an unfamiliar place is alive,
new vibrations on the ear and body:

No-see-ums, Hopsewee
Santee, Wambaw, Gullah
Black Cypress
Prothonotary Warbler
Sweet Grass
Sweet Tea
Indigo

Seek another's language,
make it familiar.
It is a fluid alchemy,
and Babel's long reverberations
beat a small retreat,
when for a moment we
are all floating down the
blackwater creek,
where fish are leaping and leaving
concentric circles
behind.

—*Adrienne Amundsen*

Magnolias by Betty Louis

Memories of My Yard

Here my fiber formed,

formed to be me

like the heartwood of a tree.

I remember early spring

after a morning rain—

the smell of young leaves

feeding the soil.

Now the spring is gone,

blossoms have turned to fruit,

the fruit has dropped

and the seeds were carried away

to come back in another way.

The trees will bloom another day

where mine will fade, forever fade away.

—Marvin Prager

Photo: Marvin Prager

Photo: Marvin Prager

Photo: Ursula Bendixen

Mepkin Abbey

Monasteries are never without visitors
—Rule of Saint Benedict, c53:16

Order of the Cistercians of Strict Observance

Mepkin Abbey, 3:15am vigils. A sky of stone,

a slab of cast iron stillness, not even a whisper of sun.

Silence, somewhere between sleep,

lucid space and the lettuce to be planted.

You begin each day in faith;

Breathe—chant. Breathe—pray.

You have complete trust the sun will rise.

Dark is temporary, stillness will be replaced.

The earth spins; it meets the sun each day.

You have faith; you observe.

You trust your part in this vast creation.

You plant your lettuce.

As human beings you occupy

a miniscule part of this universe

You take advantage of our

rare human birth to live morally.

You plant your lettuce.

—Cathleen O'Brien

At Mepkin Abbey

Ursula Bendixen

The Irish call it a thin place, a place where the barrier between this world and the beyond may allow you an opening. I looked up. I saw the vast light blue sky where gently soft, but vague clouds typical of the low country floated overhead. The sky embraced us like a giant faraway dome. We stood in a meadow; behind us a road of fine, bright white sand wound through the landscape. At the edges of the opening large old oak trees, that could easily create a tempest and fear in a storm, stood quietly like monks in an abbey. A baby oak had been born and was being baptized. I picked up the shovel; its weight was comforting, not too heavy and not too light. I felt the ridges in the wood of the handle. The blade made a satisfying crunch as it punctured the mound of earth, lifted some of it and dropped it around the base of the new tree like a minister dispensing holy water at a baptism. The thin place closed, the firmness of shovel and earth put me firmly in the here and now.

The Labyrinth

Ann Kathleen Ure

"There are no labyrinth instructions," said Father Guerric, standing in a field at the entrance to a path that was barely discernable. "You may want to walk in contemplation to the center and leave your thoughts in that space, then shed their remains as you walk back. It's about a half mile in and a half mile out." I watched my friends begin their mini journeys, Paula striding with purpose and the others at a slow, measured pace. It was a relief to follow the pack, as the path was not as clear as I'd expected. No need to make decisions I reminded myself, only to walk and to meditate.

I don't know if it was the open space, the breeze, the sun, or the birds calling from a distance that got me. It might have been the grass, the weeds, or the stray plants poking their heads above the sand. Maybe it was simply the place itself—the river alongside the gardens, the silence interrupted by prayer, the brothers' routine alongside my break in routine. But within the first hundred steps of this Mepkin Abbey interlude, the tears began to fall.

Vulnerability

Adrienne Amundsen

A word used so often in pop-psychology-drenched California that it has lost its meaning. It has become its opposite, a badge of pride for one's willingness to bare, to share, to expose.

Real vulnerability? That little fawn trembling in the bushes, tiny body curled in the grass, little head and big eyes lifted in desperate searching for mom. And she might not come back. In the timelessness of real vulnerability, fear spreads boundlessly, there is no "soon," only now, the quivering skin and silky spotted coat, trying to blend with its surroundings so you won't see.

When I peered in to take its picture I felt sorry, intrusive. I didn't want to scare it even more, only honor its rare and delicate beauty. "It's okay, little one," I whispered, but when I left, I called to friends, "Look, I got it! I got the fawn!" and showed them the pictures. This was dishonorable.

Is this what we do with our vulnerabilities, our own or each others? When what we need to do is sit quietly with the fawn, treasure the image, and pray for the return of mother?

No Questions Asked

I enter the labyrinth with the usual questions:

How will I know where to go?

What if I stray from the path?

Am I doing this right?

And the usual distractions:

What a pretty flower…

Watch that pile of straw…

Ummm, something smells nice…

Then more questions:

Am I walking too fast?

Am I thinking too much?

How do you spell labyrinth?

Until all of a sudden it just stops.

Enough for me to realize that while I don't know the way,

it doesn't matter.

The sun warms my face, and birdsong sooths my ears.

The curves and bends in the path no longer cause me

pause to question,

but encourage me to prance about.

Had I the skill to cartwheel along the path, I would do so.
Instead, I remove my shoes, welcome the grass beneath my toes,
and, shrugging off the sharp pokes of errant sticks and straw,
I wander toward my destination, smiling.

What is unknown or feared
can quickly—in less than a mile, for instance—
turn into joyous adventure,
no questions asked.

—*Paula Tevis*

How She Will Know

Approach these lips
as though they were
an assignment,
a poem   yet unwritten
take your time   study
your subject matter

begin at the heart.

With soiled
calloused hands
plant the pit of a peach
(you had to devour)

Find a hammock
overlooking marsh
(hidden behind modernity)
and wait. Wait until
you have been kissed
more than three hundred times
by the South
Remember
the burn on your cheek
the sweat of your forehead
the lash on your back
the earth in your eyes

her embrace in the dark

Take note.

And wait.

Wait for

root, trunk

branch, bud

flower, fruit.

Wait until

she is

plump, round

soft, fuzzy

juice-filled

imperfect

ready.

And then,

only then

reach up

for her

with the concise

arabesque

of an aged oak

Hold your arm in the air

until it hurts.

Do not

fill your

mouth

with her

until

Emily

Dickinson

feels physically as if the top of her

head were taken off—

and no fire can ever warm her.*

At that precise moment

these lips will know

they have been

kissed.

—Joanna Crowell

In 1870, poet Emily Dickinson wrote a letter to Thomas Wentworth Higginson, in it she explained: "If I read a book and it makes my whole body so cold no fire can ever warm me, I know that is poetry. If I feel physically as if the top of my head were taken off, I know that is poetry. These are the only ways I know it. Is there any other way?" (Letters of Emily Dickinson, L342a1870)

Blurred Borders

I.

I do not know my history

I do not know

my history

My story is still being written

My story is still being spoken

My story

is a subject-in-process

a subject emerging from the object

my great great grandmother

was branded to be

This is not my story

I attempt to read jumbled letters

but words elude me

block visual field

slip out from sieve fingers

like sand falling

one

ancient

grain

at a time

disintegrated/broken-up/mixing with earth

Like slate,

your words are layered

hard

unfamiliar to me

My tongue cannot wrap around

      My mind tangled

My soul unstirred

In your words

my soul is a myth

And now that I believe

you tell me God is dead

2.

This is not   my story

I do not recognize me

within the yellowing pages of those books

Pages crack in my palms

split skin

cut down the middle

divide me from   me

Stop yelling at me!

I am not deaf or dumb

I just don't speak your language

Your language

warned my mother

that I would come out of her womb with

zebra stripes or polka dots

Were they afraid?

Pious parishioners

afraid of my father's pale fingers

mingling between those of my brown mother

before I was even conceived of

before babies were even on their minds

My father,

the presiding minister

asked to resign.

Congregation preachin'

'bout love and forgiveness and sin

And as long as her dark skin

remained on the other side of the temple

As long as she was glued to her designated pew

she was deemed worthy

to worship with thee

If only she had remained on her knees

Sang your praises

Recited your psalms

Allowed blood to clot

If only she had not crossed red carpet

If only she had believed words

that told her she was unworthy

3.

If only he

had not come down from his pulpit

If only he hadn't held her hand

If only he had known his manifest destiny

If only he had not seen her as human

If only she had been a fetish

If only my great great grandmother

had not loaded her thirteen children

with the blood of her slave master

coursing through their veins,

onto a covered wagon

If only she had taken the money offered by his son

who followed her North to bring her back to the

plantation,

in the name of his father

If only she hadn't said,

"No, I'm going up North to Freedom!"

If only my white daddy

had buckled under the pressures

of his parishioners who warned him

not to mix the colors of the rainbow

If only

he had listened to the fears of his mother

If only she had listened to the fears of her

brothers

If only colors had remained primary

I would not be here today

telling my story

Because my story has not been written

Because my story   can only be spoken

through the mixing of colors

My story

is a rainbow blurred

and must be told through fearless

performing   free   verse

4.

My story is a poem

and it is

peacock gold

sunset orange

lemongrass green

transatlanticslavetrade blue

soft clay red

star-lit black

My story is a blurred rainbow

If you listen closely

and dare to venture

beyond your borders

you just might find your color

in my mix.

—Joanna Crowell

Landing

give me

your cheek

or forehead

or the open

stretch of

ground

between

your elbow

and wrist

on one

of those locations

I will land

—Joanna Crowell

Johns Island, S.C.

If you come to my island
in the winter, in the morning
before I have opened my eyes,
before sun has risen
from inside me

If you come bearing coffee
in a reusable ceramic cup
having received
a ten percent discount
because you care
about the earth,
and our landfills,
and your footprint

And if the coffee is hot
organic, fair trade
sweet
the right color:
me with a tan

And if you place the
steamy cup on a coaster
beside my bed,
never asking me
to open my eyes

And if I smell the fingers

of the planter, and the picker
and the roaster, and the barista

And if you follow
my no-clothes-allowed rule,
shed even your socks

And if you climb in
to the other side of my bed   cold and waiting
without exposing me   to the wind

And if you look
at my pallid   naked   face
as though it were a treasure chest
my scarf-wrapped head,
a crown
And if your hand remains silent,
warmed by the holding
of a clay mug
filled with coffee
for me
And if you reach for
my palm
instead of my breast

And if you plant your stake

in this fertile ground

with intention. Claim

your home.

Consider

your   self   ship   wrecked.

You will never be free.

—Joanna Crowell

My Love Is

sweet

as in

a fig

not straight

forward sweet

but

complex

with its unquieted

seeds

and its

female

flesh-like

open

mouth

—Joanna Crowell

Photo: Anne Woods

Art Therapy

Each painting starts
as if it's a beginning.
You hardly notice colors
flowing into one another

like a desire
trying to live in a place.
There is no wind,
no brassy sun, only

the intention of yellow
to become light.
I squint my eyes
for perspective. My brush

frees an azalea bloom
threatening to disturb the earth
with its fragile idea of pink,
releases a snowy egret.

A sliver of paint
becomes a boneless bird,
a wisp of white
for all that is fleeting.

It could have been painted with a feather.

—*Linda Annas Ferguson*

Low Tide

The rise and fall has come and gone
with the push and pull of the moon.
Soft waves unfurl, follow themselves
like measured sadness to shore.

Crustaceans, descendents
of ancient ancestors
prefer darkness, move to deep water,
their dead, dried skeletons
disappear into sand.

A heart shell, still pink inside
is half-buried by a lobster claw,
the lip of a slipper shell
embedded in a jelly fish.

I walk the shore in reverent ceremony,
collect shards of their lives,
forgive the sea its indifference.

High tide, god-like
in a gesture of grace,
will erase this wounded shore,
take back its broken things.

—Linda Annas Ferguson

The Question

Have you ever wanted to go back,
live life in reverse, watch how
a butterfly folds itself into the cocoon,
how the wet-winged fledgling
pulls the egg around itself,
seals broken edges,

feel yourself reenter the womb,
take a held breath, ride
the phoenix down into fire,
reclaim the flame of your innocence,
the red and gold ember of desire,

write your name with a hot coal
on the imperfect slate of possibility,
where everything you will ever love
already exists
complete and whole?

—Linda Annas Ferguson

Peu à peu l'oiseau fait son nid
Little by little the bird builds his nest

Labor ipse voluptas
Labor itself a pleasure

Senesco discerns
I grow old learning

*Except the Lord build the house,
they labor in vain that built it.*

Psalms 127:1 (King James Version)

Lucile MacLennan has her philosophies of life painted over the four
doors that lead from her kitchen to other rooms in her home.

Photo: Anne Woods

Montevideo

The fog, heavy as deep mourning,
Surrounded us, the ship plowing
Into the unknown, the harbor
Of sprawling Montevideo
Waiting like the lap of a mother,
Big enough to hold any strangers.

Arms waited to enfold, cheeks
To be kissed. Words whirled
Like breezes, not understood,
But felt with a wind's freshness.
Here friendliness is as real
As our pulses and courses like blood
Through the body of our meetings.
The art of life is on every street
And voices sing together in its praise.

—John Zeigler

Art washes away from the soul

the dust of everyday life.

—Pablo Picasso

History

&

Art

Photo: Sarah Wilcox

Angel of the Battlefield

Sarah Wilcox

Clara Cox pulled her thin woolen cloak tighter and peered through the flap of the medic's tent to see the small cluster of soldiers waiting for her ministrations. What had happened to the balmy winds blowing across Charleston Harbor? The chill winds blew the palmettos noisily. She was cold.

"Soldier," she said to the first in line, "come in and show me what's ailing you."

"Ma'am, I mean nurse," he said, "I've got a terrible cough and my feet are bleeding. I'm fine, I mean, no one has shot at me or nothing, but I am not sure I can march tomorrow."

She looked at him. His cheeks had the pink of either youth or fever, his uniform looked new, and in his eyes she tried to imagine she saw fear and dread.

"Turn your back to me, soldier, and let me hear you cough."

She listened and tapped his back sharply. "Catarrh," she diagnosed. "Stay out of cold rivers and sleep whenever you get a chance. Now show me those feet."

He pulled off his unlaced shoes and his knobby, knotty, grey socks. His soles were thick and callused. The tops of his feet were a different story, blistered, bruised and a little bloody.

"Who knit those socks?"

"My little sister, ma'am. She learned special so she could send me off with them."

"And the shoes?"

"Quartermaster's store, last week."

"Go back to the Quartermaster and tell him you need bigger shoes. Ask for a pair of socks, too. These are dangerous. You will be fine."

She dismissed him and motioned to the next in line. He was larger and older than the first soldier and had turned the brim of his kepi to hide the top of his face. He took the hat off and looked her in the eye.

"James," she gasped. "What are you doing here?"

"I slipped through enemy lines and crossed the Pee Dee River, just like Francis Marion. It's so disorganized here that no one has noticed me. I need to warn you. They know we've got someone here. I want to take you out."

Clara let her head sink into her hands. She didn't know what to think. A week at Fort Moultrie and she had almost begun to believe she was a nurse, a woman of the 19th century, a flower of the Confederacy.

Suddenly the flap of the tent opened with a violent snap of the canvas. A man in civilian clothes with the two bars of a lieutenant on his collar burst in, looking suspiciously at the two.

"Sir, can I help you," Clara asked. "An emergency somewhere?"

"Colonel Ripley's orders. Follow me."

"I will be with you posthaste," Clara said, worrying about both her word choice and the shaking in her hands. "Soldier," she told James, "you are well on the way to recovery. Continue using poultices on that burn, and try to keep the area clean."

James saluted the lieutenant and left the tent. Clara hoped he could melt into the busy camp without finding someone to try out his historical knowledge. It was sure to raise suspicion. He was attractive, but she was beginning to think he was a bit of a buffoon. Clara washed her hands in a basin on her camp table. She patted down her hair and tied on her grey felt hat, thinking as she did, "I'm donning a bonnet." The play-acting had caught up with her.

Photo: Sarah Wilcox

Portrait of Jack McCray by Elayna Shakur. Photograph by Jim Alexander

The Golden Age of Jazz in Charleston

Jack McCray

Charleston, S.C. entered its prime jazz age in the middle of the 20th century, coming on the heels of other periods that saw the music flourish in coastal South Carolina.

Jazz was the popular music of America until rock and roll took over in the 1960's. While Charleston was involved in the same evolution, the post-1950 period was its heyday for jazz.

Traditional players emerged from the Lowcountry's venerable institutions, Jenkins Orphanage and Avery Normal Institute, from the late 19th century through the Swing Era (1919-1945), making their mark as much around the world as they did at home, and contributing mightily to America's greatest art form, jazz music.

The Swing Era is considered by many historians as the golden age of jazz, given the popularity of the big bands, the dance crazes—such as the Lindy Hop—and the collective therapeutic effect of this hot music on the cold doldrums of the Depression.

The golden age for Charleston emerged, however, after World War II. Of course, the big bands—Ellington, Lunceford, Basie, Hawkins and others —came to the Holy City before that and Charlestonians did all the popular dances like everyone else. In fact, they invented the one, the Charleston, that literally kicked off the Swing Era. But Charleston was a relatively small market and it couldn't support resident big bands like the major cities did. There were no large hotel ballrooms or huge dancehalls, such as New York City's Savoy. There was not much of a representation of the era's typical 16-piece big band. In 1921, there was the Professor William Saxton Orchestra that was along that line but not much else.

Bebop came along in the 1940's, substantially reducing band sizes as the number of music halls and dancehalls started to decline everywhere. Also around this time, one of Charleston's most important bands, the Carolina Cottonpickers, was coming off the road. Made up primarily of former Jenkins players, it had delighted audiences in Charleston and around the rest of the country, displaying the technical proficiency and ability to swing, hallmarks of the Charleston jazz tradition.

By the 1950's, Charleston bands began to bask in the spotlight in numbers greater than ever before in the area's history. William Louis Gilliard and his Royal Sultans, the Metronome All-Stars, the Carolina Stompers, the Night Hawks Orchestra and The Royal Entertainers were among the top ensembles.

Charleston bands even had a musical style to their marketing. Gilliard worked a dance whose ticket had written on it "GET HIP! GET WISE!" then underneath "Say Diddy Bops Stick to the Jive," followed by the name of the event "A Rockin and Rollin Dance." This event was held at the Hotel James, a segregation-era mecca of black entertainment as well as a hostelry, on Spring Street near the Ashley River. It was where most black celebrities stayed while visiting Charleston.

James Hotel's Azalea Ball Room, where the standing-room-only dances, concerts and receptions were held, had a bandstand on the mezzanine level, a musical terrace, much like venues in the larger cities around the country, that marvelously filled the room with the bands' exciting sounds.

Other golden age well known venues for jazz in the Charleston area included the 52-20 Club in Summerville in lower Dorchester County; Grant Hall and the RVA Club in the Neck Area (between Charleston and North Charleston; Zanzibar, Harlem Club and Bacardi's Rose Room in North Charleston; Riverside Beach Park, a beach front pavilion, and White's Paradise, at Remley's Point east of Charleston; and downtown Charleston's Harleston Hall, Lincoln Theater, Dash Hall, Moulin Rouge, Charleston County Hall, RVA Club (later The Village), Dart Hall (also known as Dart's Dancing Casino), Colonial Cabin; Cadillac Club; Kozy Korner; Ponderosa, and the D.P.O. Hall. There were also many outdoor venues for picnics where jazz was featured as well as river cruises.

From the 1950's to the 1980's, Charleston players such as Joey Morant, Oscar Rivers, Lonnie Hamilton III, St. Julian German, George Kenny, Bob Ephiram and Raymond Rhett brought Charleston fully into the modern era. Contemporary jazz was everywhere by then.

The 1980's saw the modern live jazz landscape in Charleston come together, a scene more concert and festival oriented. Dancing to jazz had just about faded. The dances hadn't stopped but one could then go into a place to sit and just listen.

Myskyns, a membership club on South Market Street, was still going from the 1960's. Lonnie Hamilton opened a jazz nightclub on North Market Street in the 1970's featuring his band, Lonnie Hamilton and the Diplomats. Later on, it moved down the street to the second floor of the famed Henry's Restaurant.

The Spoleto Festival USA arrived from Italy in Charleston in 1977, adding a jazz series that gave Charlestonians more access to national acts. One of the Spoleto jazz series anchor venues is the College of Charleston Cistern, a greensward in the middle of the historic campus. For years, the series held popular jazz picnics at the area's historic gardens and plantations.

In 1980, Charleston's longest running jazz series until 2008, Jazz Afterhours, emerged in Piccolo Spoleto Festival, a locally produced, comprehensive, regional fest offered at the same time as Spoleto Festival USA. It was independently created for the festival by the Group for Integrated Studies under its banner "Return to the Source," also the name of the group's band led by Bob Ephiram.

The MOJA Arts Festival, a national Black arts festival, was founded by Charleston Jazz Initiative co-founder Jack McCray in 1984. Local musicians and Charleston's jazz legacy were the focus of the comprehensive festival. The national headliner was Donald Byrd, a pioneer jazz trumpeter and black art collector.

Over the years, the festivals only grew in popularity for live jazz while the local clubs faded. In the early 1980's, Reno Sweeney's opened on John Street, right around where the Charleston Music Hall is today. The Touch of Class on Meeting Street had a run from the mid-1980's to the 1990's. It was owned by Ernest Pinckney. The late Jack White, an important jazz advocate and promoter, brought many acts to the club along with Pinckney.

In the 1990's, restaurants began to be the main jazz venues. By 1992, the Chef and Clef, a three-story North Market Street eatery with jazz on the first floor and blues on the third, offered music seven nights a week.

An important Charleston percussionist, Quentin Baxter, first-call drummer for artists such as singer Rene Marie and pianist Monty Alexander, played his first professional jazz gig at the Chef and Clef. He emerged in the mid-1990's as a tour de force on the local jazz scene. He represented the next phase in the evolution of jazz musicians from Charleston. Unlike fellow Charleston drummer Alphonse Mouzon, a creative founder of the 1970's jazz fusion movement, Baxter has made a successful living touring the world while based in Charleston and playing in his hometown regularly.

Since the 1960's, a jazz industry has emerged in Charleston. There is an ever-widening talent pool and there are enough venues to sustain regular work. The city's rich musical legacy is alive and well. The golden patina still sparkles.

The Jenkins Orphanage band was in Schenectady, New York, sometime in the 1930s on a fund-raising trip.

93 Anson Street • The Heart Gate

Alphonso Brown

De Haa't Gate, (de doub'l one dey een de back oh de chu'ch) 'zine by Fulup Simmuns 'n deadekate een noneteen nihty eight wen de had de Splay'to fessva. St. Jon' duh weh Fullup Summuns go to chu'ch. 'E say'e call em de haa't gate 'cus 'e says, "'e chu'ch duh stong tuh 'e haa't." St. Jon,' bil yuh een 1850 fuh black Presaterian. Een 1861 'e blong tuh St, John Rohmun Cat'lic Chu'ch fuh de I'rish.'E clos' een 1965 'cas deh stop cum'n. Een 1971 deh St. John Rahfom 'Piscable peepul buy em.

The Heart Gates (the double gates at the rear of the church) were designed by Philip Simmons and dedicated in 1998, with a Pearl Fryar topiary garden, during Spoleto Festival. Saint John's Reformed Episcopal Church is where Philip Simmons worshiped. He came up with the "heart" design because, he says, "his church is dearest to his heart." Saint John's was built in 1850 as the Anson Street Chapel for black Presbyterians. In 1861, it became Saint John's Roman Catholic Church and served a large number of Irish parishioners. It was closed in 1965 because of a drop in membership and was purchased in 1971 by Saint John's Reformed Episcopal congregation.

(Philip Simmons was an American artisan and blacksmith specializing in the craft of ironwork. Philip Simmons is no longer among the living, he died on June 22, 2009.)

School ◆ *Paula Tevis*

From a workshop facilitated by
Master Gyotaku Artist, Sue Simons Wallace

Palmeta (Trachimotus goodei) ◆ *Sue Simons Wallace*

Dizzy by Marlene O'Bryant Seabrook

Artist Statement

Marlene O'Bryant Seabrook

I was a creative child who was constantly cutting/pasting construction paper, and began creating bulletin boards for my mother's classrooms while still in elementary school. Through the years, I learned to sew, knit, crochet, macramé, smock, cross-stitch, block straw, and felt for hats, create ceramics, and make jewelry. With each, I attained a desirable level of competency and moved on.

With no family quilters as role models, I took an eight week quilting class in 1984 with the intention of making one quilt in my lifetime. An unexpected meeting with master quilter Marie Wilson of Brooklyn, NY in 1991, led to reassessment. I have become a fiber artist who uses fabric and thread in the same manner as other artists use canvas and paint. While I have attempted several times to relegate quilting to the same fate as my other creative interests, I have not been successful. My quilts, which artistically present subjects which are of interest to me, often come to me fully colored in my dreams. They are MY gifts and no one else can interpret them as I see them. I no longer quilt just because I want to, but because I feel a creative obligation to do so.

Quilts have replaced the bulletin boards that I made as a child and as an elementary teacher early in my career. As a third generation educator, they have become an extension of my familial love of teaching and learning. It is important to me that my work be considered as more than an assemblage of colors, shapes, and fabrics. Many of my quilts involve hours of historical research before beginning the artistic design. While color and form are aesthetic necessities, the educator in me - either subtly or overtly - slips a lesson into each quilt: love of God, family, children; pride of heritage; importance of history or respect for accomplishments.

Everybody's a Critic

Myra Yeatts

The bloody shoe laid squarely downstage-center. It must have been kicked out of place by one of the set movers. I looked around. No one to ask, and I was the prop handler. What could I do? My future in theater probably depended on how I handled this. The scene would not work if the shoe was not downstage-left.

The Union officer and the Southern lady continued their heated dialogue.

"I have not seen any Confederate soldiers in months. There are no soldiers on this plantation," she said as she arched her brows and pouted.

"He was seen coming this way. Wounded as he was, he could not have gotten far. We will have to search the premises."

Oh no! Two more lines and he should find the bloody shoe at the edge of the trapdoor to the cellar. Neither of them could see the out-of-place shoe; the furniture blocked it.

Must do something, must act. Act, yes! I looked around desperately for the skirt the slave girl had discarded in Act One. I buttoned it over my jeans. I found a red dust cloth on the prop shelf and tied it over my hair. Good thing I had a two-month tan. I'd pass.

"Surely, you don't think I would stand here in front of my grandfather's portrait, the Reverend Lucus Funderburk Adams, and lie, do you?"

Last line coming up. It was now or never. Showtime.

I grabbed a broom and started sweeping my way across the stage, with my back to the full house. I began to hum loudly so the actors would see me. I heard titters of laughter throughout the audience.

They both looked at me in wide-eyed confusion.

I drawled my best Negro dialect, "It just Sissy, Miss Darla. Somebody done track up your floor wid they muddy boots. I clean it up quick as a wink." Almost there.

Jeanette, Miss Darla, skilled in improvisation, hardly took a breath before replying, "Very well, Sissy. Thank you."

My long skirt hid the action of sweeping the shoe to the appropriate location. I hummed louder to cover the sound. The Union officer's eyes popped even bigger, but he said nothing until I said, "All done, Miss Darla."

The officer looked back at Miss Darla and said his line as if the interruption had never occurred, "It would be very gracious of you, madam, if you would allow us to look around."

I stood in the wings, off-stage-left, and watched the rest of the scene unfold. The close call left me breathless, but proud.

As I expected, Jeanette was very complimentary of my own quick-thinking improvisation. She chortled happily as she swept past me at intermission on her way to the dressing room.

The Union officer, on the other hand, glared as me as he removed his gloves and placed them on the prop table. I met his gaze with surprise. What? Did he want to look like an idiot while he searched for an out-of-place shoe?

"It would have been better if you had not been humming Yellow Submarine."

There is no sincerer love

than the love of food.

—George Bernard Shaw

Food
&
Sustenance

In the Kitchen

Cindy Rasicot

David Vagasky stands in the kitchen in his white chef's coat stirring a pot of white, grainy looking cornmeal porridge. A famed chocolateier and master cake decorator, David is a multi-talented culinary artist. He currently teaches at the Pastry Department of the Culinary Institute of Charleston at Trident Technical College. He also operates his business, David's Confections, which features hand-dipped chocolate confections. To his right is a large cabbage. He cuts it into chunks and then slices those into thin slivers. On the stove is a sauté pan with vegetables and shrimp in a silky sauce. David sips from his wine glass and spins between the stove and the cabbage. To his left on the counter, he has spread out twelve golden yellow suns. "I made these tarts in the thunderstorm this morning. The doors were open and the wind blew through," he says.

The tarts are for us, a joyful group of visitors staying on Sullivan's Island. The island, three miles long, sits at the entrance to Charleston's harbor and is known for its majestic stretches of white beaches. It is also the site of a major battle of the American Revolution at Fort Sullivan (Now Fort Moultrie) on June 28, 1776. Life on the island proceeds at a relaxed and unhurried pace.

When the food is ready David serves it in ceramic bowls. The creamy cornmeal porridge goes in one bowl and the pink tender shrimp combined with red and yellow peppers and onions, goes into another. The cabbage turns into a cole slaw. "My grandmother's recipe," David says as he briskly returns to the kitchen. We all smile. David launched his own restaurant, St. Johns Island Café on Johns Island, South Carolina in 1989. In 2005 he left the restaurant to teach at Trident Technical College. He is passionate about his teaching and his business.

The creamy white cereal is grits, soon to be draped in the savory shrimp sauce. Grits, a food of Native American origin, a type of dried corn that is coarsely ground and boiled into mush. In the South, grits is commonly referred to as Geechee grits. Geechee is another word for Gullah. The Gullah people are descendants of former African slaves, primarily from West and Central Africa, living on the barrier islands. They speak their own language, Gullah, a type of Creole or modified English and maintain their own culture and culinary traditions that still survive today. Grits are eaten for breakfast and often accompany shrimp or fish at other meals. There are two types of grits, yellow and white mill corn varieties. The stone ground variety is served in fancy restaurants. In 1976 grits were declared the official state food of South Carolina. Tonight, David has served his grits with a hearty Gullah or Creole shrimp sauce.

Eleven of us hold hands around the table. Kathy, the yoga teacher and masseuse, says grace. The shrimp and grits melt in my mouth. The food is like a chorus of singing. A simple meal, beautiful colors and flavors all blended in a symphony.

"Come on out and join us," Mary Brent, our trip organizer, calls to David.

"No, I want to make sure everyone has enough to eat," he says.

We eat and talk about art and literature since we are gathered here for that purpose. The week is packed full. We are scheduled to meet with Nina Lui of Nina Lui and Friends, a Charleston Art Gallery; Karen A. Chandler, co-founder of the Charleston Jazz Initiative; Alphonso Brown who leads Gullah Tours of Charleston; Dr. Marlene O'Bryant Seabrook, an educator and fiber artist whose family enjoys deep roots in jazz; and Leigh Magar of Magar Hatworks. Writing teacher and novelist extraordinaire Linda Watanabe McFerrin is providing guidance and daily workshops about character, scene, prose and poetry. Sprinkled in are sunrise walks along the beach and ventures into the historic district of Charleston.

David comes to join us at the end of the meal. He sits by the door leading to the kitchen. He is enmeshed in his creative giving, making sure we are all taken care of. He struts around the table briskly picking up plates and clearing the dishes. As we sit basking in the sumptuous meal, David is busy squeezing whipped cream over these golden yellow orbs. He curls and winds the pastry bag expertly.

He brings out the key lime tarts and places them before us. The flavor bursts in my mouth, a tangy sweet lemon-lime flavor. It is the best key lime tart I have ever tasted. The buttery crust is a treat. But the poet in the kitchen is not finished with his song. He whisks away the plates and brings a second dessert, round mounds of chocolate cake with a dollop of creamy dark ganache on the side. My taste buds are dancing, exploding with joy.

The meal is like a dream come true, a blessing unfolding. David's attention to detail, quality ingredients, and fine cooking all combine to create magic. David Vagasky has bestowed his gifts, his grace, and his wondrous creations. We hold this cherished memory of friends sharing together, rich conversation and Southern comfort food close to our hearts.

Shrimp and Grits

David Vagasky

Grits:

Quick Grits	1 cup
Milk	1 cup
Water	1 cup
Salt	2 tsp.
Butter	¼ cup

Bring together and boil and stir for one hour. Add more water or cream as the mixture cooks out. The grits should become soft.

Shrimp:

Garlic	2 cloves
Bacon	½ pound (medium dice)
Onions	1 large (medium dice)
Green Pepper	1 large (medium dice)

Cook bacon until crisp, Add diced garlic and onions and peppers, cook until transparent.

Shrimp	2 pounds (peeled and deveined)

Add the shrimp to above and cook until pink.

Chicken stock	2 cups

Add chicken stock and bring to a boil, thicken with roux.
Salt and pepper to taste.

Roux:

Butter or oil	6 oz.
Flour	12 oz.

Combine and stir until roux coats the back of a spoon.

Pecan Pie

David Vagasky

Pastry Pie shell 9 inch

Pecans   8 oz.

Butter   4 oz.

Sugar   4 oz.

Lite Karo syrup   4 cups

Eggs   6 eggs

Bring the butter, sugar and Karo to a boil. Temper* the eggs into the hot liquid, pour the hot liquid into the pastry shell with the pecans and bake at 350 for 1 hour, or until set.

*Temper the eggs means to bring the eggs to the same temperature as the hot mixture without cooking them. Gradually add a small amount of the hot ingredients to the eggs, a little at a time, as you simultaneously whisk the mixture until all the eggs are incorporated.

Pecans

Greg Fuller

There were pecan trees in Mama Fuller's backyard in Georgia. At least three, maybe four. I don't remember exactly, but I do remember pecans always lying on the ground—sometimes more, sometimes less—just past the old wooden garage, the one with the shed roof overhanging the woodpile. There was always talk of snakes in that woodpile, although I'm not sure I ever saw one. At least not there. I'm not sure why the wood was there either, since the fireplaces in her house had long before been converted to free-standing gas stoves, another subject of perpetual caution to children. On cold mornings they would be lit—blue flames lapping out over vertical white ceramic grates, yellowed over time from use. Surely if you got too close, the flames might burn tender skin or ignite a wayward flap of clothing … and bring about tragedy.

The wood was no longer used in the washhouse across the backyard from the garage. Or even the smokehouse, long abandoned as anything other than as a place for cobwebs and to provide a residence for the collection of semi-feral cats that Mama Fuller fed each morning with small bowls of milk and kitchen scraps placed on the back stoop. Like many other things around the property, the woodpile was an antique, a vestige of a more self-sufficient farming time, no longer necessary in the modern world of Bowdon, Georgia, in the 1950s.

Not so the pecans. Quite useful as missiles to harass the array of cousins who came by during our visits, as well as some of the cats and dogs living there (I will neither confirm nor deny that fact), the pecans were put to good culinary use, baked into pies, cakes, and other treats. While we sat on the front porch, surveying the passing pickups and occasional horses and stray dogs, Mama Fuller, various aunts, and female cousins would congregate in the large kitchen on Wedowee Street to prepare fried chicken, okra with potatoes, creamed corn, black-eyed peas, or any number of other recipes handed down though generations of Fullers, Maclendons and Martins. And, of course, the pies. Pecan pies.

These were not just any pecans. No, they were Georgia pecans. There were two kinds of trees, regular and paper shell. The paper shell trees in the backyard produced a longer, more slender nut with a thinner, somewhat delicate shell that was easy to crack, making the extraction of nutmeat fairly effortless. So much so that we could pick one up, tap it against a rock, and eat the contents fresh, right out there in the backyard. They seemed sweeter than the others and were highly prized, not only for their labor saving accessibility, but also for their taste. We normally collected them as they fell to the ground, that being the indication of ripeness, although I seem to recall on a few occasions my Uncle Billy pulling a long wooden ladder out of the garage and heading up to shake the limbs and bring down even more of them, presumably to satisfy some immediate need or shortage. But that was not normal. There were plenty afoot, just waiting to be collected by the lot of us children.

A proper pecan pie—not one of the poor imitations you might find in a grocery store nowadays, lying some place too far from the origins of the nuts—is light and slightly sweet, with a fluffy butter-laden crust, pre-baked and then filled with a custard-gel-like concoction of sugar, eggs, butter and just the right amount of light Karo syrup. Atop the filling floats a solid layer of those Georgia pecans, preferably unbroken halves, lightly browned with a bit of a butter wash. It is, in my opinion, too fine a creation to be sullied by whipped cream as is often done in certain chain restaurants, or even diluted with ice cream. Unless, of course, that ice cream is of the hand-churned variety made from fresh cream, and chilled by ice, rock salt, and the labor of my cousins and me on the hand crank.

For the remaining fifty weeks of the year back up North in New Jersey, when Dad and Mom and I were not visiting Mama Fuller "down South," we felt pecan starved. I suspect pecans were available in those parts, but they were not Georgia pecans, and especially not paper shell, sweet and fresh picked from the red clay of Mama Fuller's backyard

One Christmas, a box arrived from Bowdon with a familiar PO Box return address. Inside was a homemade fruitcake, very likely a full ten pounds, tightly wrapped in foil and, as packing material, completely surrounded by …

pecans! Whole, unshelled, but paper shell no less. Just waiting to be set loose and turned into pie, as by this time, Mom had been given the recipe by Mama Fuller. Though she was still a bit of an apprentice in the pecan pie trade, Dad and I were about to task her with creating the dessert.

Every year, the much-anticipated pecan care package arrived shortly before Christmas. Apparently, during one of our summer visits, Mom mentioned that with her teaching duties, it was difficult to find time to shell the pecans, even the paper shell variety. The following Christmas, among the packing pecans (as opposed to packing peanuts), a bag full of already shelled nuts appeared. Pounds of them—all the better to bake a pecan pie.

Then another year, someone in the family (I won't say who) mentioned that the fruitcake was, perhaps, too much for our small family to consume. The next Christmas, nestled in the revered pecans, was something also thoroughly wrapped in tin foil, but taller and without a hole in the middle. It was an Amalgamation Cake!

This is a treat unique and almost beyond description, incorporating not just the sacred pecans—in this case distributed throughout with the usual sugar, butter, and egg yolks—but accompanied by raisins, arranged in layers, and completely coated with fresh coconut (most likely brought up from Florida). The fruitcake was tradition, but the Amalgamation Cake was heaven.

Until, of course, it was gone. In which case there was only one thing to do. Bake another pecan pie.

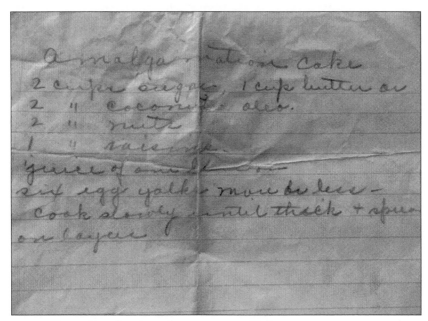

Grandma's Amalgamation Cake* • *Greg Fuller*

Cake

2 cups sugar
2 cups butter
10 egg whites
1 ½ cups milk
3 tbsp. baking powder
3 ½ cups flour
1 tsp. vanilla

Cream together sugar and butter. Sift together baking powder and flour and gradually add to sugar, butter. Add milk gradually. Add vanilla. Fold in egg whites last.

Divide mixture into two 9 x 13 inch pans. Bake in a 350 degree oven.

Filling/Icing

2 cups sugar
2 cups coconut
1 cup of butter or oleo
1 cups raisins
2 cups chopped pecans
juice of one lemon
6 egg yolks (more or less)
1 cup coconut water (or milk)

Cook slowly until thick and spread on layers of the cake.

* Note to the adventurous cook— this recipe is old and wrinkled. You may want to consult a cookbook for clarity and a more modern version!

Perhaps no bread in the world is quite as
good as Southern corn bread, and perhaps
no bread in the world is quite as bad as the
Northern imitation of it.

—Mark Twain

Gloria's Cobbler

Gloria Burg

Cobbler is the true southern dessert—top with vanilla cream, preferably homemade, or whipped cream. You may use blueberries, blackberries or peaches— even a combination of each.

Place 3 cups of berries in a square glass baking dish.

Sprinkle with cinnamon.

CRUST MIX:

2 cups self rising flour

1 tbsp. lemon Juice

1 egg

1 cup sugar

Mix these ingredients in a bowl with a fork. Then spread over the berries.

Melt one stick of butter and pour over the crust.

Bake at 350 degrees for 45 minutes or until brown and bubbly.

SERVES 6

Photos: Anne Woods

A Low Country B'al

Linda Watanabe McFerrin

If you are invited to a low country b'al in the lowlands of the South, do not get out the tuxedo and the taffeta. This is not, as I discover, a dressy affair. You might even skip the shoes.

East of the Georgia mainland, far from the urban hustle of Atlanta, from the dark reaches of the Okefenokee swamp, under the whisper of trade winds and the slow tattoo of tides, Georgia's Golden Isles drowse. Southernmost of the Sea Islands, a sweep of barrier islands that extends from South Carolina to Georgia, they are part of the long chain (at more than 2000 miles, the longest in the world) that fringes the eastern seaboard and the Gulf of Mexico from New York all the way to Texas. They shelter delicate marshlands and protect the mainland from the rages of storm and surf.

Places of lighthouse and legend, these islands have drawn and charmed visitors for centuries. Creek Indians, the Guale—their tall, naked bodies skillfully covered in vivid red and black designs—were among the first to fall beneath the spell of Georgia's Golden Isles. When 16th Century French

Explorer, Jean Ribaut, reached them, he and his men declared them the "fairest, fruitfulest and pleasantest land in all the world," foreshadowing the sentiments of those who followed. They seem the perfect place to settle in and sink roots. Spanish missionaries and early English settlers thought so. Indian middens (shell mounds) and quiet graveyards testify to tides of visitors who came—and stayed.

Bare feet sifting through sand, I walk along a shoreline dotted with sandpipers, buntings, hermit crabs and delicate, blush-colored sand dollars, as spellbound as those earlier inhabitants. I cannot think of leaving! Several yards away, Mildred DuCom, eighty-five, in her pantsuit of sea-green silk and large sun hat, wades thigh-deep through the soft, warm swells, trailing daughter, granddaughter, great granddaughter and admirers. Lawrence and I have come from two weeks of swamp explorations, finally heading east by bridges that sweep from the mainland across the Marshes of Glynn. We are on St. Simons by invitation of Mildred's daughter, Mary Brent, and Mary Brent's nieces, Shan and Mellette. We are here on a short break from all the wandering. We are here for a low country b'al.

In fact, it's not really a "ball" at all. That's the kind of trick a long, slow drawl can play. It's a "boil," a kind of bouillabaisse consisting of crawdaddies (crayfish), spices, potatoes and sweet Vidalia onions, and a southern way of serving up a welcome. An enormous pot is placed on the stove and the lip-smacking combination of "fixin's" is tossed in and brought to a boil. Other ingredients are laughter, conversation and a camaraderie that rises like the steam that billows from the giant kettle once everything gets cooking. This is a family gathering—the kind that extends to include those lucky enough to have earned the designation of "friend." Family, after all, is one of the South's most exclusive clubs; inclusion is an honor and a treat. Our hosts, ladle up the main course, an aromatic concoction guaranteed to satisfy. Several spicy bowls later, Lawrence's fiddle comes out of its case, and we all sit back to enjoy tunes like "Whiskey Before Breakfast," "Peeler Creek Waltz," and "Little Liza Jane."

Earlier in the day, the first guests to arrive, Lawrence and I had explored St. Simons and Sea Island, following oak and palm-lined avenues that seem made more for cycling, jogs, and leisurely promenades than cars. The islands wear the bright lime-green of spring—marsh grass ringing lands that once grew rice and fine Sea Island cotton. After our feast, Mildred and Mary Brent share a different side of island life with us. We go north to Christ Church where Methodist ministers, John and Charles Wesley, set the foundation of one of the first Methodist churches in the colonies. Walking thoughtfully in the quiet afternoon through the churchyard oaks, we feel a peace that settles into the bones. Formality crumbles in the heat and moisture, relaxing into a far more natural grace. Secrets emerge. And as we amble in and among the headstones, old ghosts come out to populate the stories.

The next day is our last on this short respite from a crazy state-to-state scramble, and the clan decides that we must visit Cumberland Island. We can only get to it by boat. On Cumberland Island, unlike the highly developed neighboring isles, most of the buildings are in ruins—old forts; the remains of the four-story "tabby" cottage, called Dungeness, built by the widow of Revolutionary War hero General Nathanael Greene; and what's left of Thomas and Lucy Carnegie's 19th century Plum Orchard mansion. There are no stores or businesses on Cumberland. Visitors must carry in what they need.

Marshes buffer Cumberland Island's landward side. Dunes climb inland to meet the edges of live oak forests. On Cumberland Island you might hear the bellow of an alligator in an inland pond, the warning rattle of a diamondback rattlesnake. Paths thread toward beaches on the ocean side where sandpipers, crabs and osprey dart over sand and sky and loggerhead turtles pull themselves onto the beach at night to lay their eggs. We lunch under the moss-draped live oaks, tossing boiled peanuts, "salty b'als" into our mouths and washing them down with plenty of water. We climb the dunes—a somewhat arduous task for Mildred—and we stroll along the shoreline, ears pricked to the high whinny of wild horses. One of only four barrier islands that boast feral horses (the others are Cape Lookout and Cape Hattaras off the South Carolina coast and Assateque off the coast of Maryland), Cumberland is currently home to over 200 descendants of the mustangs, appaloosas, Tennessee Walkers, and other horses transported to the islands in the early days of settlement. Wild stallions and their harems roam the dunes and forests munching on saltmarsh cordgrass, sea oats, seaweeds, and bayberry twigs. They are a beautiful sight grazing inland or galloping along the shoreline.

Our return, that afternoon, is a melancholy one, our departure imminent. There will be time for dinner, time for some fiddle music in the starlit darkness on a little boardwalk fringed in marsh grass, time to sleep and wake to a sun-drenched morning when we should set out barefoot, fishing poles over our shoulders. Instead we'll be departing, saying "good-byes" that make us feel as if we're leaving home.

It's said that when you get Golden Isles sand in your shoes the shores will call you back. I wriggle my feet as we stand at the gate preparing to leave. I rub them, brushing off the sand. Of course, I can't get it all. So I will go with sand in my shoes, a slew of lovely memories, and yes, a longing to return.

Postscript: This essay is excerpted from an article previously published in the *Rocky Mountain News* and, yes, this writer has returned—again and again—to the Southern coast.

Southern Jambalaya

Gloria Burg

1 cup chopped onion

1 cup chopped bell pepper

2 cloves garlic, pressed

1 cup cooked diced chicken

1 cup cooked diced ham

12 small link pork sausages, cooked and drained (cut in thirds)

1 pound cooked shrimp

1 cup chicken stock

1 - 16 oz. can tomatoes

1 cup raw long grain rice (Uncle Ben's)

1/2 tsp. thyme

1 tbsp. chopped parsley

1/2 tsp. chili powder

1 tbsp. olive oil

Saute onions, bell pepper and garlic in oil until tender. Add chicken, ham and sausage. Cook 5 minutes and then add all the remaining ingredients (except the cooked shrimp). Mix and put in a 13x9x2 inch casserole dish and cover tightly with foil.

Bake at 350 degrees for 50 minutes or until the rice is done and the liquid is absorbed. (Add the cooked shrimp for the last 10 minutes)

6 SERVINGS

Lowcountry Local First

"Cultivators of the earth are the most
valuable citizens. They are the most
vigorous, the most independent, the
most virtuous and they are tied to
their country and wedded to its
liberty and interests by the most
lasting bands."
—Thomas Jefferson

Beet by Cathleen O'Brien

Green Acres

Paula Tevis

Die-hard urbanites our entire adult lives, lately my husband Mark and I have been harboring the fantasy of living on a farm. The closest we've ever come to sustainable living was when we installed a compost bin in our San Francisco backyard and an errant tomato seed sprouted into an actual plant. We were thrilled even though the resultant marble-sized tomatoes were few and not that tasty. Sadly, I can't even be relied on to water the houseplants regularly.

So what are we thinking? That away from city life there's a place with clean air, quiet lanes, bird song, and a plethora of fresh vegetables and eggs a short stroll from the back porch? That future grandchildren will have room to roam in the summers and fruit trees from which to pluck ripe nectarines? I'm not even sure where these ideas come from. Yet now and then, my dear spouse will email me pictures from real estate sites of acreage in the countryside and we will earnestly discuss just how much land we'd need for a few goats, the chicken house, and a proper kitchen garden. And the answer to these questions is... how the hell would we know?

The reality check that will likely keep me safely ensconced in the city was a delightful visit to Thornhill Farms, a "show farm" near McClellanville, South Carolina, population 491. In fact, this place epitomizes the urbanite's dream of rural life with adorable piglets following about like puppies, docile mother lambs nursing their newborns, and row upon perfect row of heirloom vegetables exclusively grown for the hippest Charleston restaurants. Even the farm shop appears to be plucked from a 1940s film set. Owner Maria Baldwin, an exile herself from the big city, was recovering from a fall during my visit, so tour of duty fell to Matt, the produce manager. Matt, who appeared to be in his twenties, is tall, with long brown curls, straight white teeth, a milky complexion, and the chiseled features of a Banana Republic model. Central casting did a cracking good job recruiting this boy out of Ag school.

My group of gone-to-seed writers and artists blithely followed Matt around in the rain, picking organic strawberries at his invitation, admiring his growing practices, and nodding in agreement as he described the intricacies of irrigation. Though enthralled, I still noticed his damp socks inside black Crocs caked with mud. Dirt freckles cascaded down his shins and his khaki cargo shorts needed laundering, badly. Somewhere by the eggplants (or were those potatoes), two dewy young interns holding hoes gamely attempted to control the many, many weeds interspersed among the young plants. The girls waved and smiled at us, sweet pleading smiles from faces hopeful that someday they, too, might be free to walk away from their labors, dry off, and drive somewhere for a nice dinner. Another couple of twenty-somethings underneath a shelter used some clever implement to form small dirt bricks in which to start seeds. They resembled happy seven-year-olds playing in the mud, but all I could think was, "This looks like a lot of work."

Once we'd admired the three acres of cultivated land, Matt passed us over to the livestock manager, a slim, blond, bearded fellow in torn Levi's who would make a divine Marlboro Man if cigarette ads were still lawful. Nate oversees the pigs, sheep, chickens, and the lone cow. His affection for the swine was particularly beautiful to witness, although he doesn't let emotional ties get in the way of his fondness for bacon. Nate explained to us his belief that meat eaters ought to witness the kill, also known as "processing the animals," in order to make an educated decision about consuming animal protein. Perhaps. But I, too, would prefer not to let emotions get in the way of my dinner.

We then left the pigs to their handsome forest pen, me guiltily picturing pork belly, and obediently followed Nate to the pasture where the chickens and sheep are kept, surrounded by four movable enclosures. There were three flocks of around 500 generic-looking, big-breasted white birds of varying ages, aimlessly hanging about like bored teenagers lacking imaginations. The birds have about eight weeks to enjoy themselves in the fresh air, pecking the dirt should they so desire, before bidding the farm adieu and heading off to the processors. Their more attractive brown cousins—in separate five-star accommodations farther off in the field—lay the eggs the farm sells for $4 per dozen. Nearby, about ten newborn lambs nuzzled their moms, the males destined for roasts and chops, the females for reproduction. I wondered how Nate managed to move the netting needed to fence in the chickens, as well as the enclosure for the sheep and the cow, which he did quite regularly in order to give them fresh pasture. I wondered when he was going to get to leave for his own home as it was already late in the day and he'd spent over an hour with us, an hour that might have gone to better use.

Exhausted by this time, merely from trekking around the farm, my own shoes and socks damp from the rainfall, mosquito bites aching for a scratch, I got into a car ready to head into McClellanville for dinner at the village's sole restaurant. With time to contemplate, I asked myself if my desire to eat fresh eggs and pick my own salad for Sunday lunches was heightened or squelched by an afternoon at Thornhill. Well, that depends obviously, on how many wide-eyed farm interns I can find to work the land.

Thornhill Farms, photo: Marvin Prager

"Herb Rap" for Fun

My favorite foods are herbs and spices.

They often make a food that entices.

Try a few sprigs of rosemary

or a lemon verbena potpourri.

Go to sleep on lavender-scented 'pilla'

Even the cat sniffs nepitella.

Put your mint and booze in the blender.

Basil pesto keeps you regular.

Chamomile and valerian tea - mellow.

Calendula cleanses and blooms yellow.

Get smarter and clearer with melissa.

Thyme would really miss ya'.

So you better eat! Taste the Flava'.

—Kathy China

Okra Fried Rice

Alluette Jones Smalls

This dish has been in the Singleton family since I began to know myself. July is when the okra pods show their fuzzy faces around town, so we prepare fried okra, sauteed okra, okra soup, okra as a french fry but the best treat of all....the Okra Fried Rice.

4 tsp. olive oil

2 pounds okra sliced

3 oz. red pepper chopped

3 oz. onions chopped

pinch of cayenne pepper

4 cups cooked organic brown rice

4 tbsp. wheat free tamari sauce

1 cup chopped tomatoes

Pour olive oil into skillet heated to medium, then add the next four ingredients. Saute until al dente (about 3 minutes). Add the rice and tamari sauce, and blend. Garnish each serving with fresh tomatoes.

MT. ZION AME CHURCH
FASTING SUGGESTIONS

FAST from judging others;
   FEAST on Christ dwelling in them.

FAST from fear of illness;
   FEAST on the healing power of God

FAST from words that pollute;
   FEAST on speech that purifies.

FAST from discontent;
   FEAST on gratitude.

FAST from anger;
   FEAST on patience.

FAST from pessimism;
   FEAST on optimism.

FAST from negatives;
   FEAST on affirmatives.

FAST from bitterness;
   FEAST on forgiveness.

FAST from self-concern;
   FEAST on compassion.

FAST from suspicion;
   FEAST on truth.

FAST from gossip;
   FEAST on purposeful silence.

FAST from problems that overwhelm;
   FEAST on prayer that sustains.

FAST from worry;
   FEAST in faith.

Shrimp and Grits at the Mt. Zion AME Church

Kitty Hughes

We sit in a room off the Mt. Zion AME Church sanctuary. The adjoining wall is inset with a ten-foot-or-so stained glass window. Frozen in a welcoming posture, Jesus beams down on us, transferring celestial hues of gold, carmine, and royal blue to our tables.

The tables are long, Formica-topped fold-ups lined horizontally under the window, offering a continuous view of Jesus, who will darken and disappear as late afternoon gives way to night. I wonder if Jesus gets hungry looking down from up there. Wouldn't you get hungry if you had to gaze down on steam trays brimming with local fare: creamy grits, okra sauteed with tomatoes, and chicken smothered in onions? I try to imagine all of the offerings that Jesus will never taste but seems to be enjoying vicariously.

Laura Brown and Evelyn Smith, the church members who cooked this evening's meal of shrimp and grits, graciously share their recipes with me. For the grits, measure one cup of grits to three cups of water and simmer. You can add sour cream, milk, or cheese toward the end, the secret of the creamy texture. For the shrimp, saute bell peppers and onions, and brown Hillshire smoked sausage separately in a side pan. Remove the bell peppers and onions from their pan and cook the shrimp in the same pan until pink. Put it all together and then add the gravy, salt, and pepper.

We don't have time for the gravy recipe, but I would call it a roux, probably made with flour and pan drippings. I love its rich, reddish-brown color. I taste the South in this dish, the terroir. I feel the women's hands preparing it for us; feel their pride and the loving lavishing of their time to make it.

In the church foyer, I pick up a list of fasting suggestions for Lent. It's a long list: fast from judging others, fast from discontent, fast from bitterness, and other pretty good reminders. I am glad that "fast from eating homemade South Carolinian specialties" is not on the list. I am sure Jesus would approve.

Hugh's Shrimp & Grits

Hugh China

Ingredients:

1 cup Asiago cheese

1 cup stone ground yellow grits

1 1/2 cup diced cured ham (sugar or salt)

1/2 cup onions, diced

1 cup green bell pepper, diced

garlic to taste, diced

1 cup plain flour

3 tbsp. clarified butter

6 to 8 shrimp per serving

6 cups rich chicken broth

crushed red pepper

cayenne pepper

Cajun Seasoning

1. Prepare grits according to instructions. When done, add cheese to taste, stir, add butter to taste.

2. In sauce pot melt butter. When melted add flour. Allow to brown, stirring as needed until it reaches a dark brown color. Remove from stove, allow to cool for about 2 minutes. Slowly add the broth a little at a time, mix with a wire whisk to fully incorporate and continue mixing until all liquid is in.

3. Return pot to stove, allow to cook slowly, stir to prevent film from forming. Do not allow to boil, cook slowly for forty-five minutes.

4. Meanwhile dice ham, garlic, onions and bell pepper. Place in a separate sauce pot, cook slowly until onions are clear. Remove from heat.

5. When sauce is done, it should be a smooth texture, not thin. If too thin, thicken with a mixture of broth and flour, add a little at a time until it reaches your desired thickness.

6. Using a double strainer or cheese cloth, strain sauce into pot with ham/onion mixture. Return to stove on low heat. Season with crushed red pepper, cayenne pepper and Cajun seasoning to taste. Keep hot.

7. Cook shrimp using desired method. Place grits in a bowl, top with shrimp and then sauce.

Thornhill Farms, photo: Cheryl Armstrong

Pickled Pig's Feet

Pickled pig's feet
parked their car
next to a mayonnaise jar

Having gone hither and yon
their non-existent toes
were drawn

To that big glass home
that once held cukes
where now they would
hang up their Dukes

—*Billy Vandiver*

Country Ham with Gravy

Charlotte Jenkins

Serves 4

Use red-eye gravy with country ham. The red eye is adding a touch of coffee to the mix. I guess it keeps your eyes open. A Southern thing.
—Charlotte

2 tbsp. vegetable oil

4 (1/4-inch thick) slices country ham, about ½ pound

¼ cup chopped onion

Dash granulated garlic

Dash black pepper

¼ cup all-purpose flour

1-1/2 cups chicken stock

1 cup black coffee

Heat the oil in a skillet until hot but not smoking. Add the ham and fry for about 4 minutes on each side. Remove the ham and set aside. Add the onions, garlic and pepper to the skillet and sauté for 5 minutes, or until the onions are tender. Add the flour and stir over medium heat for 5 minutes, or until the flour has turned light brown. Stir in the chicken stock, bring to a boil, reduce heat and briskly simmer, stirring frequently for about 10 minutes, or until the liquid thickens. Stir in the coffee and briskly simmer for 5 minutes, stirring frequently.

Return the ham to the skillet and simmer for 5 minutes. Adjust the seasoning, if desired. Adjust the consistency by adding a little more chicken stock if it is too thick.

Serve over grits or grits spoon bread.

From Charlotte Jenkins' book Gullah Cuisine: By Land and By Sea,
Evening Post Books, Charleston South Carolina

Sampling the South with Writers: Try the Crab Balls!

Martha Dabbs Greenway

As a South Carolina native, I've been a sampler of fine Southern cuisine for many years, and as one of the founders of the Southern Sampler Artists Colony, I was thrilled to be sharing that cuisine with a great troupe of writers joining us for our Eat, Play, Write April writers retreat. Having set up, along with SSAC co-founder Mary Brent Cantarutti, an unusual and far ranging culinary tour, I was looking forward to dining at T.W. Graham & Company Seafood Restaurant, an eating establishment in McClellanville, South Carolina. In fact, T.W. Graham & Company is the only restaurant in McClellanville… and it is enough.

We had just finished Bud Hill's walking tour of this small coastal shrimping village with its population of only 491 and were delighted when Bud joined us for dinner, never pausing in his stories about the town he loved. Bud told us that the original owner of the building in which the restaurant is situated was a man with the improbable name of Buster Brown. Apparently, Buster lived by the philosophy of not following the usual rules. Bud pointed toward the vacant lot next door and explained that Buster had expanded the building way beyond its present location. The only flaw in this ambition? Buster didn't own the land. In addition, he installed the septic tank on yet another property he didn't own.

But that was yesteryear. That night I ate the best crab balls I'd ever eaten. Although I was born and reared in the South, I had never heard of crab balls—crab cakes, yes, crab balls, no. About the size of a good meatball, they were fresh, light, with just the right spices—large enough for maybe two or three bites, but tasty enough to gulp down in one. Bud proudly related that they had been written up in *Bon Appetite*. I should stop here and explain that T.W. Graham & Company was originally a general store and still retains many artifacts from its past; this is not a fancy white-tablecloth-and-flickering-candle upscale place. No, it is at best called "rustic".

When one of our party spotted fried green tomatoes on the menu, it brought memories of the 1991 movie, *Fried Green Tomatoes*, starring Cathy Bates and Jessica Tandy. Laughing at shared passions, my travel companions and I ordered a plate for the table. Crisply fried, the firm green tomato retained enough "bite" to make it a tasty treat. Since some of our group came from California, this was a new experience in Southern cuisine. The next course was a delicious carrot and ginger soup topped with a crostini and a small yellow flower. I ate it all.

It was a good thing one dinner partner and I decided to split the shrimp platter. It came in a traditional red plastic basket. Carefully placed on a bed of mesclun greens sat twenty-five perfectly fried shrimp that must have been swimming in the ocean that very morning. Sweet potato fries, cole slaw and hush puppies completed the meal. We almost cleaned the plate, and I'm certain my satisfied smile indicated to us both that we had indeed eaten at the best restaurant in town.

Paula's Oyster

It was Paula's first oyster on the Carolina shore.
She gulped it down. Anton asked, "More?"

"Oh, no." She smiled, "It fit the bill.
I think perhaps I've had my fill."

She was far too polite to spit it out
'though the grit in her teeth felt like grout.

Instead she waited 'till the wine was poured,
'till the captain said the boat was moored

and she raised her glass to make a toast.
"Next time," she said, "let's have a roast

of oysters cleaned of their silty bed.
We'll pack a meal planned way ahead

of crabs and shrimp, hush puppies, cole slaw,
ice tea to drink—maybe a nude to draw.

With Cathleen at the helm and Karen on hand
our feast will quickly draw a jazz band."

—*Martha Dabbs Greenway*

It Came In the Mail

Jim Martin

It came in the mail today. At that very moment, time stood still. Nothing the second before mattered. Getting lost in the pages felt no different than it did when I was eleven.

Only then it was a Burpee Seeds catalog. The anticipation of spring, color, and the absence of cold toes and fingers made going to the mailbox bearable. The catalog was the prize of the day and I had won.

Annuals, big seeds planted in cardboard egg crates and basking under grow lamps, made spring come quicker. I didn't know what an annual really was. They just grew fast and flowered as summer started. They died before the pumpkin foliage turned brown. Most times, they returned the next year.

One of my favorites was a zinnia called Candy Stripe. The catalog pictures didn't lie. It produced handfuls, enough to see from a distance and just as many to cut and carry indoors to mom. If they ever had powdery mildew like they do here in the Lowcountry, I've imagined it gone. The near perfect foliage, apple green and blemish free, led the eye to the cheery multicolored petals.

There won't be much snow today, slowing my walk to the mailbox. Cardboard egg crates have been replaced by fancy propagation flats and engineered soil mixes. I now know the definition of an annual. Everything is different.

Or maybe it isn't. Senorita Pink glows brightly as she is revealed through the opening in today's mailbox. I can't keep my eyes off of her, a sure sign of an early spring.

Mint

Sugar

Bourbon

Ice

yum!

Mint Juleps

Louise Bevan

Put sprigs of fresh mint (4 to 6 leaves) into a glass.

Sprinkle with powdered sugar and just a bit of
water to dissolve sugar.

Muddle or bruise leaves and fill
glass with finely crushed ice.

Add another mint leaf or two on top, fill glass with
bourbon of your choice and place in refrigerator for a
minimum of an hour, two or three hours better.

*I don't always measure exactly, depending upon how much
mint and/or bourbon I have but generally go by the recipe.
I noted that the dictionary says it is to be taken along with
or instead of medicine. I prefer the latter.*

Photo: Anne Woods

Photo: Catthleen O'Brien

Hold a true friend with both your hands.

—Nigerian Proverb

Acknowlededgements

Many thanks to the contributors and the

many writers and artists who join us every year

in a celebration of life and place.

Special Thanks

To **Michael Haga**,

Associate Dean, School of the Arts

College of Charleston,

who paved the way.

Photo Collage: Tim Mitoma

Michael Haga Unveiled

Michael Haga is like a priceless brandy,

Smooth as silk and apt to make you randy.

His taste is for expensive knickernacks

He buys from Nina Liu's exploding racks.

He is our Southern-doodle-dandy.

—John Zeigler

Photo: Karen Chandler

To **Karen Chandler,**
Professor in Arts Management,
College of Charleston,
and co-founder of the
Charleston Jazz Initiative,
for the music.

Photo: Billy Vandiver

To **Nina Liu,**
owner of Nina Liu and
Friends Gallery,
for sharing her large
circle of friends.

Photo: Ursula Bendixen

To **David Vagasky,**
Chef Instructor, Pastry
Department of the Culinary
Institute of Charleston at
Trident Technical College
for setting a place at his table.

Heartfelt thanks to: Linda Watanabe McFerrin for teaching us to weave words. Cathleen O'Brien for designing *A Southern Sampler* and the talented team of editors—Cheryl Armstrong, Mary Brent Cantarutti, Kate Crawford, Martha Dabbs Greenway, Linda Watanabe McFerrin Gail Strickland, Julie Thompson, Ann Ure, Sarah Wilcox and Anne Woods.

South Carolina Friends

Billy Vandiver • Michael Haga • Karen Chandler

Valerie B. Morris • Robert Russell • John Zeigler

Mary and Stephen Glickman • Mary Boyd • Sue Simons Wallace

Alphonso Brown • Nina Liu • Linda Ferguson • Shari Stauch

Merry Thoe • David Vagasky • Jim Martin • Alluette Jones Smalls

Charlotte Jenkins • Nikki Seibert • Anton DuMars

Joanna Crowell • Torreah "Cookie" Washington

Quentin Baxter • Robbie Scotts • Harriet and McIver Watson

Maria Baldwin • Marc Rapport • Arthur McDonald

Father Guerric • Judith Kramer • Kathie Livingston • Casey Price

Charlton Singleton • Marlene O'Bryant Seabrook

Selden B. Hill • Ivy Moore • Bobbi Adams • Mary Tuggle

Gloria Burg • Janna McMahan • Paul Holmes

Carla Damron • Don Ubben • Louise Bevan

W.A. "Billy" Dabbs • Tommy & Evelyn Dabbs

Dick Dabbs • Brenda Remmes • Phil Tuggle

Grainger McKoy • Karen Watson • Alice Boykin

Pearl and Metra Fryar • Susan Lentz • Laura Spong

Elielson and DeAnne Messias • Hugh China

South Carolina Beautiful Places & Smiling Faces

SSAC Meanderings

Swan Lake Gardens
Sumter

Pearl Fryar Topiary Gardens
Bishopville

Boykin Mill Pond & Grist Mill
Rembert

Sparkleberry Swamp
Rimini

Sumter County Gallery of Art
Sumter

Vista Studios
Columbia

College of Charleston Campus
Charleston

Magnolia Cemetery
Charleston

Fort Moultrie
Sullivan's Island

Nina Liu and Friends Gallery
Charleston

Gibbes Museum of Art
Charleston

Charlestown Landing
Charleston

Colonial Dorchester State Park
Summerville

Bull's Island
Awendaw

Mepkin Abbey
Moncks Corner

Hampton Plantation
McClellanville

Hopsewee Plantation
Georgetown

Avery Research Center
Charleston

Gullah Tour with Alphonso Brown
Charleston

Home and Studio of Philip Simmons
Charleston

Tideline Tour with
Captain Anton DuMars
Folly Beach

Thornhill Farms
McClellanville

Shem Creek
Mt. Pleasant

Jeremiah Goat Farm & Dairy
Johns Island

Magar Hatworks
Charleston

Nathaniel Russell House
Charleston

Aiken-Rhett House
Charleston

Alluette's Cafe
Charleston

Gullah Cuisine
Mt. Pleasant

Kayaking Wambaw Creek
Nature Adventures Outfitters
Mt. Pleasant

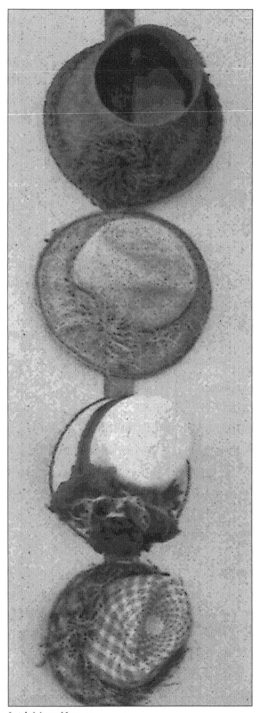

Leigh Magar Hats

Writers, Artists & Chefs

ADRIENNE AMUNDSEN is a southerner by way of Texas, though she has lived in California since the fabulous and turbulent late 60s. She is a psychologist practicing in San Francisco and San Rafael. Her interests have taken her from the Paleolithic cave art in France to International Women's Day in Afghanistan. Her book of poems, *Cassandras Falling*, was published in 2010, and she is working on a compilation of poems about her trip to Afghanistan. She is married and has two grown sons.

CHERYL ARMSTRONG is a San Francisco Bay Area writer, photographer, certified yoga instructor, and world traveler. Her career was spent as an automation librarian in academic, public and special libraries. She was a Peace Corps volunteer in Ethiopia and a librarian in Istanbul, Turkey. Cheryl writes about outsiders and what they teach us about ourselves.

UNITY BARRY graduated from the San Francisco Art Institute, but after she worked for way too long in the corporate world, she retired to write about her favorite subjects—artists and Paris during the Gilded Age. She recently finished her first historical novel, *Luminous—Berthe Morisot and the Birth of Impressionism* and is starting her next about Mary Cassatt. She was a short-listed finalist in the 2011 William Faulkner-William Wisdom Writing Competition and has two short pieces in the anthology, *Wandering Paris* due out in fall of 2013.

URSULA BENDIXEN was born in California, but is a true citizen of the world. She lived in Brazil, Portugal and her ancestral home, Germany. She now lives in San Francisco, where she co-owned a graphic design studio, learned the ancient craft of glass blowing, and studied painting at the Legion of Honor Museum. An avid photographer, she loves to turn her lens on Charleston and South Carolina wonders.

When **MARIANNE BETTERLY** isn't hip hop dancing, photographing Buddhas or searching for cappuccinos in Kyoto, she's writing poetry. Her poetry has been published widely in books and journals, including the *Hot Flashes* series, *The Green Silk Journal*, and *The Haight Ashbury Literary Journal* among many others. Marianne lives in Kensington, California.

LOUISE DABBS BEVAN, the beloved Mayor of Dabbs Crossroads, South Carolina and a strong advocate of highways devoid of litter and excess signage, received early assertiveness training by standing her ground with five brothers—three older and two younger. Her interests include restoration of historical sites, musical performances and lively conversations. She has a degree in music from Duke University with further training at Jullliard School, and serves as a substitute organist at Salem Black River Presbyterian Church, Mayesville, South Carolina.

GLORIA BURG, an interior designer born and raised in Columbia, South Carolina, began her love and fascination with cooking in the late 60's. Coming from a family of good cooks with Lebanese and Greek heritage, it was natural to branch out into other cuisines—French and Italian from a life of travel and southern from her roots. Gloria has had cooking classes with Jacques Pépin, Marion Sullivan and Nathalie Dupree.

ALPHONSO BROWN, born and reared in Rantowles, South Carolina, a rural area outside of Charleston, South Carolina, has received numerous degrees, but is perhaps best known as the director of five choirs and the band at Mount Zion AME Church, and his Gullah Tours of Charleston. The author of *A Gullah Guide to Charleston*, Alphonso charms natives and visitors who want to discover the "real" Charleston.

Born, bred and reared to be a fan-carrying lady, **MARY BRENT CANTARUTTI** headed west in pursuit of romance and adventure. She never lost her drawl. Co-founder of the Southern Sampler Artists Colony and writer of Southern Women's Fiction, her inner compass points toward cooling Atlantic breezes.

KATHY CHINA lives in Sumter, South Carolina with her husband, two horses and a Siamese cat. Born and raised in North Dakota, she moved to Sumter after college to pursue a career in law enforcement, serving primarily in the Mounted Patrol Division. Her segue into massage therapy, fitness training, and yoga instruction has occupied the last thirteen years. A few years ago, Kathy began to write her first novel in the loving arms of the Southern Sampler Artists Colony.

HUGH CHINA was born and raised in Sumter, South Carolina, where he currently lives with his wife and best friend, Kathy, two horses and a cat. Retired from the US Army and the City of Sumter's Police Department, he pursued his dream—cooking and owning his own restaurant. *Voila!* The Café on Main, downtown Sumter, where Hugh whipped up made-from- scratch Southern delicacies with a twist—many inspired by his mother, Thelma.

KAREN CHANLER, Associate Professor in Arts Management at the College of Charleston, received her Ph.D. in Studies in Arts and Humanities from New York University, M.A. in music education from Columbia University-Teachers College in New York, and B.S. in music education from Hampton University. From 2001-2004, she served as director of the College of Charleston's Avery Research Center for African American History and Culture. Co-founder of the Charleston Jazz Initiative, a multi-year study of the jazz tradition in Charleston and South Carolina, Karen has been widely recognized for her passion and dedication to the arts, including being presented the 2010 Preserving Our Places in History Individual Award by the South Carolina African American Heritage Commission.

JOANNA CROWELL is the founder of Ascension Theatre and the Women Writing from Experience workshop series in Charleston, South Carolina. A professional actress for over twenty years, she has performed her own poetry across Canada and the United States. A strong advocate for women, social justice, and peace, she is the author of the choreopoem *Double Dutch: What are you so afraid of? Jump in!* and the play *AWOL: A Soldier's Journey.* Her first collection of poems, *I Ate a Rainbow for Breakfast,* was published in 2012. She currently resides on Johns Island, South Carolina.

SOPHIE DABBS (1900-1983) and ELIZABETH DABBS THOMPSON (1898-1975), were sisters who grew up together and parted for only a brief time to attend college. They returned to Dabbs Crossroads to live their entire lives in the same house with one another. Sophie was a breeder of Rhode Island Red chickens, grew vegetables, and prepared "soul food" for family and friends while Elizabeth cared for the cats, planted mimosa trees along the highway, and baked the best coconut cake ever. Educators, they were both members of a local metaphysical society that studied extra-sensory perception, paranormal phenomena, and hypnosis.

JAMES MCBRIDE DABBS (1896-1970) was a soft-spoken philosopher, who began his career as an English Professor at Coker College, Hartsville, South Carolina, but returned to his ancestral Dabbs Crossroads to write and farm. His legacy as a prominent advocate for civil rights and racial equality continues to be recognized internationally. In addition to copious writings, he authored *The Southern Heritage, Haunted by God, Who Speaks for the South*, and *The Road Home*.

GUY MCBRIDE DABBS (1904-1983) earned his BA in Liberal Arts at the University of South Carolina and received a certificate in music theory and composition from Peabody Conservatory. A gentleman farmer and gifted musician, he played the piano, organ, guitar and violin and composed classical music. He also grew tobacco that was over six feet tall and helped his two sons cultivate prize-winning yams that were recognized by President Harry Truman.

ANTON DUMARS, a thirty-three year resident of Folly Beach and a US Navy submarine veteran, serves as a geology adjunct professor at the College of Charleston and a Coastal Scientist for Tideline Consulting, LLC. Mostly, he likes showing off the South Carolina salt marsh to guests aboard his tour boat, "Tideline".

LINDA ANNAS FERGUSON is the author of five collections of poetry including, *Dirt Sandwich*, published by Press 53; and *Bird Missing from One Shoulder*, published by WordTech Editions. A native of the Carolinas, she lives in Charleston, where she shares the marsh with egrets, language, art, and other living things.

GREG FULLER writes personal essays and humorous accounts based upon his experiences in everyday life. Although raised North of the Mason-Dixon Line, his Southern family roots reach deep into Georgia, Alabama and Tennessee. A graduate of Vanderbilt University, Greg now lives in Sausalito and Lake Tahoe, California. Look quickly—you may see him gliding across the bay under sail, struggling to maintain verticality on the slopes, or on the streets, trailing behind Max, his Golden Retriever.

MARTHA DABBS GREENWAY is a seventh generation South Carolinian, and resides at Dabbs Crossroads in a rambling country farm house built by her granddaddy. Co-founder of Southern Sampler Artists Colony and retired Director of the Sumter County Cultural Commission, Martha lives contently with her two cats, Sonoma and Rafael, rescued on the Northern California coast—and a third cat, an orange tabby named Salem, who showed up on her porch, while she was reading about an orange cat dropped off at a library in Iowa.

MICHAEL HAGA, native of the Commonwealth of Virginia and Associate Dean at the College of Charleston School of the Arts, received a Master of Arts and Liberal Studies degree from Hollins College in Roanoke, Virginia. In addition to his administrative duties, Michael teaches art history, currently serves on the board of the South Carolina Arts Alliance and chairs the International Council of Fine Arts Deans' Advocacy Task Force. An avid art collector and traveler, he judges and reviews art exhibitions locally and beyond.

KITTY HUGHES has an insuppressible passion for preservation and place. She writes regularly for the Oakland Heritage Alliance newsletter and has two essays forthcoming in 2013 in *Wandering in Paris*, one of which is an essay about Gertrude Stein in Paris and Oakland. She has also been published in *Wondrous Child, The Joys and Challenges of Grandparenting* (North Atlantic Books). Kitty's as yet untitled novel-in-progress, set in New Orleans and Oakland, was a semi-finalist in the 2011 William Faulkner-William Wisdom Writing Competition.

CHARLOTTE JENKINS, chef and owner of Gullah Cuisine in Mt. Pleasant, South Carolina, has been cooking Gullah foods since she was nine years old, but it wasn't until she moved to New York and started entertaining guests in her home that she realized there was something special about her Gullah culture. A 1988 graduate of Johnson & Wales School of Culinary Arts, Charlotte says it's "food that speaks to ya!" Judging from the rave reviews in *The Washington Post, NY Times, Gourmet and Southern Living,* plus the long lines at Gullah Cuisine, folks are listening!

For almost twenty-five years, NINA LIU—"Queen of the Arts"—has used her Charleston-based gallery, Nina Liu and Friends, as a platform for championing and promoting the visual arts, especially contemporary art by South Carolinians. A uniquely talented ceramicist, she was a leader in the development of the French Quarter Gallery Association and the establishment of the French Quarter Art Walk. The South Carolina Arts Commission chose Nina for the 2011 Elizabeth O'Neill Verner Award in the category of Business.

BETTY LOUIS is a native Californian, born and raised in the Napa Valley. After many years heading fashion and production at Levis Strauss and Co., she is now a Master Botanical Artist. Her watercolors have been exhibited throughout the San Francisco Bay Area.

Legendary JACK MCCRAY, a native of Charleston, received his B.S. degree from Shaw University, and a M.A. degree from Central Michigan University. For twenty-five years, he edited copy, wrote columns, reviewed books, and reported sports, general news and features for Charleston's Post and Courier daily newspaper. Founding president of Charleston's MOJA Arts Festival, started in 1984, he co-founded the Piccolo Spoleto Festival Jazz Afterhours series, and from 1980 until 1989, produced and hosted black music programs on WSCI-FM Radio, the NPR affiliate in Charleston. Co- founder of the Charleston Jazz Initiative, Jack authored numerous publications including Charleston Jazz.

LUCILE MACLENNAN, born in Hartwell, Georgia, shared her parents and grandparents' love of plants. An inspiring 92 years "young," she has devoted decades to the study of native South Carolina plants, and has over 300 collected specimens growing in her garden. A member of the Charleston Garden Club for forty-nine years, she is renown for her writing, speaking engagements, tours, and educational programming. In 2010, she was the recipient of the 1830 Award, presented by the Charleston Horticultural Society in recognition of her commitment to botanical pursuits that has further enriched the greater Charleston horticultural community.

JIM MARTIN, a lifelong gardener, who has worked for twenty-one years on a variety of public horticulture projects in South Carolina, including the development of the nationally recognized ninety-acre Botanical Garden at the Riverbanks Zoo in Columbia. A graduate of Clemson University with a bachelor's degree in ornamental horticulture, he is currently programs director of the Charleston Parks Conservancy. In addition to horticulture, Jim enjoys floral artistry, writing and photography. He lives on James Island, where he tends his own half-acre garden.

LINDA WATANABE MCFERRIN is an award-winning poet, travel writer, and novelist. Her latest novel, *Dead Love*, was a Bram Stoker Award Finalist. Linda has judged the San Francisco Literary Awards, the Josephine Miles Award for Literary Excellence and the Kiriyama Prize, served as a visiting mentor for the Loft Mentor Series and been guest faculty at the Oklahoma Arts Institute. A past NEA Panelist and juror for the Marin Literary Arts Council and the founder of Left Coast Writers®, she has led workshops in the U.S., Greece, France, Italy, Ireland, Central America, and Indonesia.

San Francisco Bay Area native **TIM MITOMA** started drawing at age four and never stopped. At various points in his life he has done advertising and editorial illustration, graphic design, merchandise design, bicycle graphics, and fine art. In the rare moments when he's not drawing something he can be found riding his bike, writing children's stories, or searching for enlightenment in the refrigerator.

CATHLEEN O'BRIEN is a fifth generation Californian and book designer by profession. She fell in love with the South in college when she read Flannery O'Connor's *A Good Man is Hard to Find*. Her newest passion is botanicals, which she captures on paper with pencil and watercolors. Can there really be 50,000,000 cells in a single leaf?

MARVIN PRAGER, a.k.a. Marv, is often found in his native habitat of Marin— the little gem nestled between San Francisco and the Wine Country—moving with meditative grace amidst flora and fauna. Readily identified by at least two Apple devices on his person, Marv is a fifty-year resident of Marin and has been a docent at Angel Island, the San Francisco Conservatory of Flowers, the San Francisco Botanical Garden, and Muir Woods. Besides being a natural science encyclopedia on legs he is also an adept artist, photographer, and indefatigable hiker.

CINDY RASICOT is a free-lance writer, former psychotherapist, and adoptive mother living in the Bay Area. She was raised on black-eyed peas and fried chicken in Aiken, South Carolina. Although her family moved to California when she was ten, she still shares a love of all things Southern. She currently blogs at her website, www.talkinghearttoheart.org, a supportive community for parents raising adopted teens

BRENDA REMMES writes and breathes near the Black River Swamp—fertile soil for her most entertaining characters. She returned to South Carolina after fifty years of hopscotching across the USA to create something other than grant proposals and education workshops. What she's doing now is a lot less meaningful but more fun.

DR. MARLENE O'BRYANT SEABROOK, whose family's roots extend deep and wide into Charleston jazz history, is also a well known educator and gifted fiber artist. Having made history as The Citadel's first African American professor, she became fascinated some twenty years ago with art quilts. One of forty-four nationally recognized fiber artists invited to create a quilt honoring President Obama for an inaugural exhibition at the Washington Historic Society, Marlene travels extensively to lecture about her work. There's always a portable sewing machine nearby!

ELAYNA SHAKUR loves her recent focus on paintings from outer space, which she creates based on Hubble photographs, but her heart belongs to portrait art. Since she was a four-year-old, Elayna has been fascinated with the human face, and feels honored to paint the likeness of someone—especially a person she admires—who has passed over to another dimension of life. Strongly connected to spirit, her paintings are often thought to enhance appearances, but according to Elayna, any enhancement is because she sees her subjects without judgment.

ALLUETTE JONES SMALLS is an entrepreneur, chef, educator, fashion model, philanthropist and cancer survivor. She is the owner and executive chef of Alluette's Café in Charleston and a native Charlestonian. She holds a bachelors degree in education/history from Savannah State University, Savannah, Georgia. A practitioner of the "Slow Food Movement" and "Farm to Table", she credits her being cancer-free to educating herself about the effects of foods on the body, daily exercise, relieving stress, non-conventional medicinal practices and her belief in God.

PAULA TEVIS, a native of Santa Barbara, California, and a wanderlust at heart, now lives in London, where she takes singing classes, produces pop-up entertainment, knits an occasional sweater, and conjures up divine dinner parties. She mothers from a distance, and in between, writes.

ANN KATHLEEN URE lives in the San Francisco Bay Area. Throughout her varied career she has written advertising copy, product fliers, song lyrics, grants, business proposals and first-person essays. Her travel stories have been published in the anthologies *Floating through France: Life Between Locks on the Canal du Midi*, *Venturing through Southern Greece: the Vatika Odysseys*, and in the magazine, *France Today*.

CHEF DAVID VAGASKY's passion for the culinary arts evolved from his Minnesota heritage. A 1986 graduate of the Culinary Institute of America, David was introduced to the tantalizing world of chocolate during his internship at The Greenbrier resort in White Sulphur Springs, West Virginia. In 1989 David opened St. Johns Island Café on Johns Island, South Carolina, a popular full-service café with an in-house bakery. Sixteen years later, he left the restaurant business to teach in the Pastry Department of the Culinary Institute of Charleston. An educator and chocolatier extraordinaire, David enjoys the slow paced, Lowcountry lifestyle.

A native of Charleston and a graduate of the College of Charleston, BILLY VANDIVER is retired from a career in education at both Trident Technical College and the Medical University of South Carolina. He likes nothing more than walking the historic cobblestone streets and settling in to for a good read at one of Charleston's hospitable coffee/tea shops. His special interests include acquainting visitors with the city's history, gardens, and architectural diversity; enjoying its many incredible restaurants and cultural offerings with friends and most recently—dabbling in creative writing.

SUE SIMONS WALLACE is a direct descendant of Benjamin Simons, a Huguenot, who settled on the Cooper River near Charleston in 1693. Sue, an artist and renowned supporter of the arts in Charleston, has always been fascinated with reflections and impressions of objects. In 1990 she discovered gyotaku (fish rubbings). From the carefully chosen handmade Japanese rice paper to the finest inks, and freshly caught fish, Sue delights in making impressionistic, fossil-like images that are correct but not exact. Uniquely collectible, Sue's gyotaku work has been exhibited across the United States.

TOREAH "COOKIE" WASHINGTON is a studio fiber artist, activist, rabble rouser, mother and friend living in Charleston, South Carolina. Cookie's art quilts focus on the divine feminine. Cookie wants her art to move, challenge, and inform the viewer. She is not at all interested in making art that matches your couch.

ANNA ELIZABETH WATSON was born on October 29, 1979, in Charleston, South Carolina. She graduated from the University of North Carolina in Chapel Hill in May, 2002. Her passions were the arts, spiritual pursuits, animals and loving people. She passed away on June 24, 2011.

SARAH WILCOX is a San Franciscan who enjoys both time and space travel.

ANNE WOODS is a commercial pilot and flight instructor. A third generation pilot, she soloed a glider on her fourteenth birthday. Anne is passionate about antique airplanes and flies a 1932 Waco biplane and a 1946 Cessna. She has a Bachelor of Arts in English from the University of the Pacific. Her short story, *Riding the Wave*, about a glider pilot, was a finalist in the 2011 William Faulkner-William Wisdom Creative Writing Competition. Her articles have appeared in Pacific Flyer and In Flight magazine. Two of her travel essays were published in *Venturing in Southern Greece: The Vatika Odysseys*. She lives in the San Francisco Bay Area.

MYRA YEATTS wears her Southern culture with both pride and irreverence, a paradox that often defines her writing. She teaches English at the University of South Carolina Sumter.

JOHN ZIEGLER, 101 years "young" and celebrating, is a Charleston legend. He and his partner, Edwin Peacock, owned The Book Basement, touted as Charleston's favorite bookstore for three decades. Both men were personal friends of Carson McCullers, who used to visit them at John's beach house on Sullivan's Island. In addition to *Edwin and John*, a book about the forty-nine year relationship with his partner, John wrote two books of poems, *Alaska and Beyond* and *The Edwin Poems*. A longtime supporter of the College of Charleston's School of the Arts, John was awarded a honorary doctorate degree by the College in 2012. The South Carolina Arts Commission named John the recipient of the 2013 Elizabeth O'Neill Verner Award in the category of Lifetime Achievement.

44772662R00114

Made in the USA
Charleston, SC
06 August 2015